About the author

Fiona Jeffries is a Vancouver-based res‹ and currently a visiting scholar at the C‹ in Culture and Communities at Simon F‹............ ....y. ncr work focuses on the multiple expressions of contestation to the globalization of fear, particularly in spaces of migration and border crossing, in cities recovering from civil war, and in spaces of tourist development and ecological degradation. She has published extensively in both academic and journalistic venues, focusing on feminist politics, media and gender violence, urban social movements, and the role of communication practices in the production of alternative globalizations.

NOTHING TO LOSE BUT OUR FEAR

FIONA JEFFRIES

IN CONVERSATION WITH LYDIA CACHO, GUSTAVO ESTEVA, SILVIA FEDERICI, DAVID HARVEY, JOHN HOLLOWAY, WENDY MENDEZ, SANDRA MORAN, MARCUS REDIKER, AND NANDITA SHARMA

ZED BOOKS
London

Nothing to Lose but Our Fear was published in 2015 by
Zed Books Ltd, 7 Cynthia Street, London N1 9JF, UK

www.zedbooks.co.uk

First published in Canada in 2015 as *Nothing to Lose but Our Fear: Resistance in Dangerous Times* by Between the Lines,
401 Richmond Street West, Studio 277, Toronto, Ontario M5V 3A8

www.btlbooks.com

Cover designed by Dougal Burgess

A catalogue record for this book is available from the
British Library

ISBN 978-1-78360-415-9 hb
ISBN 978-1-78360-414-2 pb
ISBN 978-1-78360-416-6 pdf
ISBN 978-1-78360-417-3 epub
ISBN 978-1-78360-418-0 pdf

Printed and bound by CPI Group (UK) Ltd, Croydon, CR0 4YY

MIX
Paper from
responsible sources
FSC www.fsc.org   FSC® C013604

To my parents

CONTENTS

ACKNOWLEDGEMENTS

Like a book, conversation is irrepressibly social, and, for me at least, one of life's supreme joys. Although not every conversation has a resolution in the end, almost any dialogue is energized with the sense of possibility, clarification, and discovery. Conversation helps us work through problems—think anew. It is habitually cited as a tonic for loneliness, anxiety, depression, and despair. This book tries to bring the social and collective character of thinking about and challenging a world awash in fear into sharp, if imperfect and always unfolding, relief.

First off, I would like to shower unreserved thanks on the people who made this book possible: those willing conversationalists you will meet in these pages who set aside considerable time and energy in order to engage in these discussions. Soon after I began this project, I made a decision to carry out these dialogues with people whose work does not directly pivot around fear itself, and my co-conversationalists greeted this challenge with verve, solemnity, and great generosity.

I would need another volume, which I don't have, to sufficiently acknowledge the many people who provided me with an inordinate amount of concrete support, joyful encouragement, and bracing criticism. Pablo Mendez, Zoe Druick, and Barbara Pulling spent countless hours talking through the questions and concerns woven through these pages. Pablo's input at every stage of this project was immeasurable, and I cannot thank him enough for his seriousness and loving generosity. Mike Ma, Kirsten McAllister, Samir

Gandesha, Yuezhi Zhao, and Dorothy Kidd have all been immensely supportive in innumerable ways. Dorothy Christian, Jules Boycoff, Saskia Sassen, and Alex Rivera offered invaluable space and time to grapple with core questions.

I researched and carried out several of these conversations while I was a visiting scholar at the Center for Place, Culture and Politics at the City University of New York Graduate Center. David Harvey, Neil Smith, Padmini Biswas, Mary Taylor, Jenna Loyd, Malav Kanuga, Tatiana Schor, and the other "fellows" at the Center ensured my time at CUNY was intellectually electrifying. The exemplary open-heartedness, social generosity, and political commitments of Silvia Federici and George Caffentzis nourished me daily. A scholarship from the Social Sciences and Humanities Research Council of Canada enabled me to live, pay the rent, and learn more than I could have imagined.

Warm and heartfelt thanks to my Mum (Diane) and Bill, my sisters Diana, Sandra, and Catriona, and to Kate, Sally, Marty, and Thomas. Much appreciation to Lew, Carla, Kestrel, Maryann, Eric, Harold, Louise, Steve, Carmen, Julie, Fen, Sharla, Andrew, Winnie, Janeth, Nandi, Gaye, John, TJ, Ruth, Harjap, and Shannon for sustaining the friendship commons. I can't imagine the world without this collectivity of conversationalists!

Much gratitude to Jessie Hale for her thoughtful and patient editing, and to Amanda Crocker, who is not only an impressive and super-competent editor, but, like everyone else I've encountered at Between the Lines, a confidence-inspiring delight to work with and a heartening exemplar of what committed independent publishing looks, feels, and acts like.

INTRODUCTION

T HE CONVERSATIONS featured in this book took place over a period
of intense planetary upheaval. I started to conduct interviews for this
project in 2007, amid the first stirrings of what turned out to be a
global financial crisis. The Wall Street meltdown of the following
year spread out rapidly to all continents, injecting a blast of hot fear
and anxiety into a world already reeling from the disorienting grind of neoliberal excising, roiling wars, and spirals of depressive disaffection and violent
dispossession. In response to the crisis, governments began to impose a new
round of punishing austerity, unleashing major rollbacks in social spending
and protections but also dramatically increasing expenditures on weapon-
ized "public safety." This global drift into neoliberal security has been deftly
exploited by right-wing political entrepreneurs, who have sought to profit
from the generalized climate of anxiety by seizing upon people's proliferating fears: the fear of loss of status and national pride, of unemployment
and homelessness, and more generally of a future becoming inexorably fore-
closed. In Greece and the United States, as in many other places, a resurgent
right has sought to present itself as a heroic camp of rebels fighting an unjust
order, harnessing popular fears by viciously scapegoating anyone who could
be recast as the dangerous source of popular misery. But starting in 2010, mass
protests against authoritarianism and manufactured scarcity began to rum-
ble across the aggrieved streets and plazas of Tunis, Cairo, Athens, Madrid,
Hong Kong, New York City, Toronto, Istanbul, Mexico City, and many other

places, and have since continued to unfold across the world. As these uprisings gather momentum, a systemic critique of the use of fear as a tool of social control has grown louder and louder. Have ordinary people lost their fear?

One answer to this question is suggested by the mainstream and alternative news coverage of the early days of the uprising against Egypt's authoritarian neoliberal state in 2011. In clip after clip featuring the protesters gathered in Cairo's Tahrir Square, one can hear women and men of all ages characterize their presence in the streets and the square in terms of a popular victory over fear. "The wall of fear came down!" protesters repeatedly exclaimed. And while the scale of these new uprisings may be unprecedented, the sentiment is not unique to our historical moment. We may be living through a revolutionary epoch, but in the long and tumultuous history of political resistance to arbitrary power, these periods of popular outpouring become again and again witness to the wall of fear toppling down.

This book brings together an international group of scholars, artists, and activists with whom I have discussed a question that has risen to prominence over the last decade: How can we think critically and act productively in a world awash in fear? The conversations you will find here offer reflections and provocations from a variety of perspectives and experiences to help us understand the current global uprising against fear in new ways.

For decades, inquiry into the subject of fear has focused on the threat political fear poses to democracy, and more generally to the Enlightenment ideal that reason should prevail over emotion. More recently, the discussion has been shaped by two of the past decade's signal events: the 9/11 terrorist attacks on the United States, and the global financial cataclysm of 2008. For sociologists, filmmakers, media critics, and philosophers, the intensity and unprecedented reverberations of these traumatic events suggest that we have entered a new age of global fear. Scholars, journalists, and artists have launched a renaissance in "fear studies" as they try to understand the strange, irrational, and cruel behaviour human beings can eagerly come to embrace when overwhelmed by fear.

Long before today's proliferating fears came to dominate media headlines, scholars of modernity—from Baruch Spinoza to Karl Marx to Frantz Fanon to Hannah Arendt—recognized the centrality of the politics of fear to both the exercise of power and the entrenchment of hierarchies. In the 1990s, with the ascendancy of the neoliberal form of capitalism and the proliferating antagonisms unleashed by the end of the Cold War, the political implications of pervasive social fear became a preoccupation of sociologists, filmmakers, journalists, philosophers, and futurists. Up until this point, the dominant Anglo-American analyses of fear tended to treat it as an individual psychological affliction, rather than a site of political power and struggle. But the ascendancy of neoliberalism in the 1990s was accompanied by a notable shift in critical thinking about fear's political and cultural significance. As an economic and political project devised and elaborated upon by elites determined to retrench the social gains won by the great emancipatory struggles of the last two centuries, neoliberalism ushered in a period of aggressive deregulation, privatization, and marketization. As anyone seeking access to welfare, childcare, housing, environmental protection, or labour rights can tell you—and as capitalism's global economic crisis of 2008 made wrenchingly clear—for a growing number of people around the world, this neoliberal turn made life increasingly precarious. And as life for many became increasingly insecure and wealth ever more concentrated, a growing number of studies revealed how fear is deployed as a technology of political discipline. We have seen this coercive use of fear unfolding across everyday life, such as in the devastating escalation of incarceration in the US and the paradoxical trend towards open markets and militarized borders, whose lethal consequences play out daily on the US-Mexico border and the Mediterranean Sea. We find it in metastasizing surveillance and the proliferation of increasingly elaborate modes of political repression. Researchers examined, for example, the role of narratives that dominate global neoliberal culture—personal responsibility, do-it-yourself social uplift, and virtuous sacrifice—and how they render invisible the very arrangements that make many people's lives increasingly precarious, dangerous, and insecure.* How can we not

---

* Of the writers working on the politics of fear in the 1990s, the urbanist Mike Davis has been among the most prominent. His influential books *City of Quartz* (New York: Vintage, 1992) and *Ecology of Fear* (New York: Vintage, 1998) analyzed what he saw as the authoritarian implications of an increasingly fearful world. Sociologist Barry Glassner's bestselling book

be fearful in a globalizing environment full of systemic insecurities, such as falling wages, growing numbers of zero-hour contracts, clawbacks in social services, spiralling food prices, and soaring inequality? Other researchers** focused on the dominant neoliberal media culture and the way it effectively turns our legitimate fears against us by trading on stories about statistically remote threats, such as terrorist attacks or flesh-eating disease. The weight given to such fears, social critics like Barry Glassner and Mike Davis have convincingly argued, distracts people from the systemic source of their insecurities while further empowering fear mongers in politics, the commercial media, and the booming global security industry.

One important branch of this literature documents how a new geography of fear is a catalyst for the aggressive reorganization of cities around anti-crime and counter-terrorism planning and governance, often through the

---

The Culture of Fear: Why Americans Are Afraid of the Wrong Things (New York: Basic Books, 1999) deliberated on fear as an explanatory tool for understanding North America's zeitgeist on the eve of the new millennium. Soon after his book was released, Glassner's fear thesis was featured prominently in Michael Moore's hit documentary *Bowling for Columbine* (Beverly Hills: United Artists, 2002). In the aftermath of September 11, 2001, a flurry of books on political fear appeared, including Paul Virilo, *The Administration of Fear* (Cambridge, MA: Semiotexte, 2012); Michael Laffan and Mex Weiss, eds., *Facing Fear: The History of an Emotion in Global Perspective* (Princeton, NJ: Princeton University Press, 2012); Slavoj Zizek, *Living in the End Times* (New York: Verso, 2011) and *Violence* (New York: Picador, 2008); Hugh Gusterson and Catherine Besteman, *The Insecure American: How We Got Here and What We Should Do about It* (Oakland: University of California Press, 2010); Wolfgang Sutzl and Geoff Cox, *Creating Insecurity: Art and Culture in the Age of Security* (New York: Autonomedia, 2009); Uli Linke and Danielle Taana Smith, *Cultures of Fear: A Critical Reader* (London: Pluto, 2009); Susan Smith and Rachel Pain, *Fear: Critical Geopolitics and Everyday Life* (London: Ashgate, 2008); Derek Gregory and Allen Pred, *Violent Geographies: Fear, Terror and Political Violence* (New York: Routledge, 2007); Susan Rotker, *Citizens of Fear* (Chapel Hill, NC: Rutgers University Press, 2002); Joanna Bourke, *Fear: A Cultural History* (Berkeley: Counterpoint, 2007); Corey Robin, *Fear: History of a Political Idea* (Oxford: Oxford University Press, 2006); and Zygmunt Bauman, *Liquid Fear* (Cambridge, UK: Polity, 2006).

** Sarai Media Lab, *Fear* (Delhi, India: Centre for the Study of Developing Societies, 2010); Steve Goodman, *Sonic Warfare: Sound, Affect and the Ecology of Fear* (Cambridge, MA: MIT Press, 2010); Steve Macek, *Urban Nightmares: The Media, the Right and the Moral Panic over the City* (Minneapolis: University of Minnesota Press, 2006); David Altheide, *Terrorism and the Politics of Fear* (New York: Rowman and Littlefield, 2006).

importation of changing techniques of warfare. Another branch has emphasized the role of a hyper-concentrated and competitive mass media environment in the authoritarian circulation of fear, as news and reality television increasingly trade on the spectacle of bleeding bodies, zones of abjection, and interpersonal crime. An additional area of research has centred on the role of right-wing demagoguery in the propagation of fear as a strategy to shore up brittle regimes and impose consent by force.

Nothing to Lose but Our Fear touches on these various dimensions of the culture and politics of fear. However, it also tries to grapple with how fear works, not only as an emotion and as a tool of the powerful, but also as a dialectical relationship. Fear certainly signals oppression, domination, and—as many scholars have convincingly argued—a debilitating sense of helplessness. But precisely because it is political, fear ought also to be understood as a catalyst to, if not a site of, a range of individual and collective forms of refusal and resistance. To critically consider this dialectic, *Nothing to Lose but Our Fear* uses a dialogic format to bring together a series of reflections about contemporary and historical manifestations of our much-discussed "culture of fear." The conversations take place at a bewildering conjuncture whereby metastasizing security—justified all over the world in the name of fighting terrorism and crime—meets with mounting socio-economic and existential insecurity, justified as the imperative of neoliberal rationality. This overwrought setting initiated my desire to converse with others about fear's significance for politics, and specifically for emancipatory politics, today.

Two main concerns set the practical and theoretical foundation for this project: first, a desire to understand political subjectivity in a context of accelerated accumulation by dispossession; and second, a sense of the pressing urgency to reflect on the ways in which fear has crept into the social fabric, stealthily chipping away at people's capacity to extend social generosity or solidarity. Accordingly, I have entered each discussion in the spirit of dialogue and in search of radical critiques of fear as a political problem. My questions were driven by a craving to move beyond the more typical way in which fear is understood politically as a tool of top-down manipulation. To this end, I have sought to pay close attention to how fear is contested in a variety of dangerous and fear-saturated spaces—including sites of extreme gender violence, spaces of migration and border crossing, places that have been pounded by political violence, and cities recovering from decades-long civil wars. The conversations seek to provoke consideration of the often hidden histories of people's emancipatory practices and ideas.

Hence, my aim is twofold. First, the book seeks to provide an insightful and provocative set of reflections on the question of how a climate of generalized fear poses a perilous barrier to democracy, freedom, and social justice. More specifically, I am interested in creating a space for reflection in the company of others on the ways in which pervasive social fear stunts people's capacity, both mental and material, to care much about those outside of one's immediate orbit. The social fear that dominates neoliberal modernity has proven to be indispensable to conducting and justifying its attack on long-struggled-for initiatives of collective welfare, however incomplete, fragmentary, and problematic these might be. The rollback of the welfare state, the erosion of redistributive notions of justice, and the increasingly repressive policing that has accompanied this double movement almost everywhere have effectively increased people's sense of vulnerability and fear. Therefore, the social fears considered in these dialogues cannot easily be adjudicated along a trajectory of reason and irrationality, as a number of sociologists and journalists insist, because such fear is a reasonable corollary to a social system that idealizes competition and the creative, generative powers of scarcity. Indeed, the governing social and symbolic environment is so drenched in the dogmas of privatized life, individual responsibility, and malicious competition that the corrosive fears these values engender are often invisible to the naked eye. In response, this book seeks to provide an alternate lens for looking at our contested present.

But the conversations I have gathered here do not simply dwell on the myriad of ways in which social fear operates as an oppressive force and a technology of top-down power. Instead, they seek to refocus our thinking towards a dialectical understanding of how fear moulds, but also antagonizes and transforms, political subjectivities. This aspect raises the book's second and arguably more important goal, which is to identify the various ways in which social fear is resisted in a wide range of places, times, and circumstances. Rather than seeing the contemporary culture of fear as a monologic, all-consuming technology of total power and control, the people interviewed in this book think about fear "from below." That is, they approach it from the perspective of the protagonists of culture and from the point of view of social antagonism. The interviews therefore bring into focus the ways in which fear is resisted, and in so doing they point to the fragility that is inherent in relations of domination.

As such, the conceptual backdrop to these dialogues rests on three key features. The first is an emphasis on forms of popular resistance to the politics of fear. Putting the accent on contestation helps us move beyond the "culture of fear" discourse that is prevalent in contemporary academic debates and popular media, and that inadvertently occludes any sense of the existence of such antagonism. In different ways, the conversations you will find here trouble the unidirectional and totalizing approach to thinking about fear by focusing on the experiences and reflections of scholars, artists, and activists who work outside of the "fear studies" framework, but who are actively engaged in or with spaces where fear is a dominant feature of everyday life. Second, by raising the visibility of critique and resistance, the dialogues shed new light on the relationship between political subjectivity and fear. The conversations in this book reject a position typically found in many journalistic and sociological analyses of fear, which often designate people's fears as irrational because they are based on imagined threats; from this perspective, people simply need to draw on the force of reason or an appropriate understanding of probability and statistics to overcome this problem. But rather than reducing fear to an irrational emotion, the contributors to this book point to various ways and contexts in which people have acted against political fear—in spite of their fear. Third, by bringing together grassroots activists and politically engaged scholars, *Nothing to Lose but Our Fear* offers a different way of thinking about the historic and contemporary role of political courage in public life and in emancipatory struggles.

The experiences, thoughts, and feelings expressed in this book provide brilliant insights into the urgent question of social or political fear, but because the interviewees do not work specifically on the subject of fear, most of these insights have not been published elsewhere. The interviews with the many widely read authors found in this collection present ideas about the problem of fear that remain unavailable to the many readers who follow their work. Readers interested in fear studies who may not have encountered these authors will appreciate the original and thoughtful approaches they offer. Furthermore, the collection lies side by side with the ideas and experiences of grassroots social activists and acclaimed scholars, providing a unique combination of voices and lucid, exciting conversation.

The conversations, particularly those conducted with social activists working in dangerous places, also engage in an exploration of political courage. What comes across very strongly here is that political courage does not signify the absence of fear, as many treatments of the topic have unwittingly implied. Rather, the discussions reflect on how, at certain moments, the political uses of fear from above fail to exert their power over people's capacity to challenge them. For example, the interviews with political activists Sandra Moran, Wendy Mendez, and Gustavo Esteva uncover a way of thinking about and acting in contexts of extreme fear and insecurity, where collective actions and solidarity are emphasized over individual acts of heroic fearlessness. Hence, this collection of conversations provides the vital perspective of resistance that has heretofore been largely absent from the wide-ranging debates about fear in politics and culture.

Finally, the book provides a unique perspective on the relationship between the micro and macro levels of experience. Fear itself is a passion that reverberates across the personal and the political. It is a "natural" human emotion, felt at the level of individual bodies and mental conceptions. Fear is also a manifestly collective affect that echoes across the social body. Thus, an exploration into how we live amid and against our fears demands that we dissolve the separation between the micro and macro or personal and political. I ask my interviewees to reflect on their involvement in various movements and relate this to the wider context of the global "culture of fear." Each conversation therefore combines personal experience with systemic analysis of structural processes that affect people's lives. The conversation form is uniquely suited to drawing such connections. This format also provides another way of thinking about inspiration in a context where bookstore shelves heave with the weight of volumes advising us to reckon with our fears in order to overcome them, as though our fears were independent from the political, economic, and socio-cultural environment in which they are cultivated, circulated, and acted upon.

The nine conversations in this book are organized into three main sections: Historicizing, Theorizing, and Practicing. The authors interviewed in the first section cover a range of fear-infused events that were central to the making of the modern experience, including the practices of terror and mercy on the trans-Atlantic slave ship, the witch hunts in Europe and its colonies, the oppressiveness of fascism in the Second World War in Italy, and nineteenth-century panics about the urban crowd. In the section devoted to theorizing fear, the conversations resonate more closely with the existing literature by conceptualizing fear as a technology of power. The interviewees share their insights and expertise on the role fear plays in the organization of urban life, in moments of political repression, in the mass media, and in the world's proliferating and militarized border zones. Finally, the third section turns towards the practice of resistance to fear in spaces characterized by acute insecurity and violent conflicts. Interviewed here are activists, journalists, and artists whose work seeks to intervene directly in spaces of fear, succeeding in the process to interrogate, overturn, and even laugh at fear and its otherwise dreadful embrace.

This book seeks to offer a contribution to the planetary uprising against fear. We know that the fear mongers quickly set to work on reassembling their most effective and time-tested weapons of political power, coercion, and consent. But as the discussions collected here make clear, the moments of conversation, listening, and mutuality that often characterize political encampments and ongoing revolts of the discontented and the dispossessed can produce outpourings of collective courage that persistently chip away at the seemingly impenetrable fortress of political fear.

— *Fiona Jeffries*

PART I

HISTORICIZING

1

MARCUS REDIKER

The Theatre and Counter-Theatre of Fear

MARCUS REDIKER is an historian of the sea working in the "history from below" tradition. A Distinguished Professor of History at the University of Pittsburgh, Rediker is known for his animated histories of early modern piracy, slavery, and plebeian rebellion. He has devoted many books and articles to uncovering hidden histories of resistance in the making of the modern world. Like his predecessors (the social historians C.L.R. James, Christopher Hill, and E.P. Thompson), Rediker is interested in uncovering the protagonist role of those who have been systematically written out of the historical record: slaves, sailors, and other anonymous commoners. He has powerfully shown, for example, how pirates of the early modern era built radical alternative forms of social organization in opposition to the brutal conditions that prevailed in the merchant marine and the British Navy. These sailors-turned-pirates sought both to escape their violently exploitative condition as workers in merchant and naval ships and to create alternative, less authoritarian ways of living collectively.

Rediker's writing on early modern pirates, slaves, sailors, and waterfront political culture recalls hidden histories and lexicons of global resistance, and his work has influenced contemporary debates about globalization and the struggle for autonomous mobility. In our discussion, Rediker relays extraordinary stories of rebellion and multi-racial cooperation amid the extreme terror and proliferating antagonisms that formed the dramatic, if so often concealed, historical backdrop of global modernity. He relates this bottom-up historical approach to his own experiences of the segregated US South and to his activist work with the movement to abolish the death penalty in the US.

Political Formations

FIONA: Your books are filled with interesting characters that are largely written out of mainstream accounts of the histories you explore: piracy, early modern globalization, the waterfront, merchant shipping, and Atlantic slavery, to name just a few! Can you tell me about some of the events and experiences in your life that nourished the ideas you explore in your writing?

MARCUS: I would start with my family background. My parents are from poor, rural families of Tennessee and Kentucky, and I grew up in that part of the world. My grandfather was a coal miner and a storyteller. He was a big influence on the way I write history. I came of age in the late 1960s and early 1970s, amid the various social movements of the times. Then I spent several years labouring in a factory in Richmond, Virginia, where I really began to think about the world. So it's a combination of a working-class background and the generational experience of the sixties and the seventies.

FIONA: You are an historian of the sea, and one of the ideas that seems central to your work is the idea of the ship as an early factory. What about your own experience working in such a factory? Did the conditions there inspire an understanding of factory work that continues to percolate in your writing on working-class history?

MARCUS: In that factory of thirty-five hundred workers, I became interested in questions of race and class in American history, and in working-class history more broadly. In my section of the factory, tensions ran high among three generations of workers. An older group was all white, a group of middling age was mostly white, and the younger generation, in their late teens and twenties, of which I was a part, was the most racially mixed group. My two best friends in this group were devotees of Malcolm X, and in our area another man was a Grand Wizard of the Ku Klux Klan. Racism was heavy and fistfights often broke out in the cafeteria. I began to think seriously about why, even though we shared the same boss and working conditions, we would rather fight each other than fight those who wielded power over us. Although I should also mention that we did battle the bosses, especially through struggles to control the pace of work. The guy who trained me on a machine was skilled at causing it to break down so he could take long periods of rest. He was class conscious in that sense, but at the same time he was an extreme racist. He liked to call me "nigger-lover."

After I was laid off from that job, I got a straight day job, which allowed me to take classes in night school at Virginia Commonwealth University, one of the biggest night schools in the country, with open admissions and cheap tuition. I took two classes, one on the American Revolution and one on the Russian Revolution. This is where my formal interest in history began.

FIONA: Would you say that those early workplace experiences were as formative as the particular debates about history that you encountered in the university?

MARCUS: I would say more. It was growing up in the South, dealing with ever-present questions of race and class. But the factory experience was crucial, and in retrospect I can see that I have basically been working on the race and class theme ever since. I worked and went to night school, and when I finished my undergraduate degree I decided to go on to graduate study. I wanted to study slavery's role in Caribbean and American history. I ended up moving in a different direction, towards work at sea, once I began my studies. But the race and class questions stayed with me.

FIONA: How do pirates fit into that?

MARCUS: Accidentally. When I got to graduate school, I was interested in work being done in England by historians around E.P. Thompson. They were using legal records to reconstruct the histories of working people who didn't leave any records of their own. They had recently published a book called *Albion's Fatal Tree: Crime and Society in Eighteenth-Century England*. I wanted to do that kind of work—history from below. I happened to choose as a research topic sailors and pirates. I didn't know anything about seafaring. I grew up in landlocked Tennessee, so it wasn't out of a love of the sea that I did it. Rather, it was because I thought I could find documentation about the lives of these people, and that proved to be the case. I basically became a specialist in Atlantic and transnational labour history by choosing to study seafaring people. I just followed them around wherever they went.

FIONA: Did you see a kind of continuity with the figure of the sailor and your factory experience?

MARCUS: I saw the sailor as a worker from the beginning—a worker who had an intense experience of being confined on a ship. I also found that most labour histories at the time (the 1970s) didn't have room for sailors. They considered sailors "marginal." The emphasis fell instead on white, male, skilled workers, so I took it as my task to try to bring the common sailor into labour history. When I told people what I was studying, they would say, "Oh, you study those quaint, marginal people." I would bristle and say, "Marginal to what? Certainly not to the worldwide accumulation of capital." What they were saying was that sailors were marginal to a landed, national history, even to the labour history version of the same. I wanted to write Atlantic history with sailors at its centre.

Histories of Violence

FIONA: One of the things associated with sailors, and especially pirates, of the early modern period is violence. Can you talk about how you see the role of violence in the making of the modern world?

MARCUS: When I started my research (in what was then the London's Public Record Office, now The National Archives of the United Kingdom) and began going through court records about sailors, I found, lying on top of a stack of documents in a box, this long, black something-or-other. I couldn't tell what it was. I put it aside and began to read, and what I found was that this was a piece of hemp that a sailor had brought in as evidence—his captain had beaten him nearly to death with it. The blackness was his long-dried blood. So I had this surreal introduction to the violent world of the deep-sea ship. By accident, this instrument of torture and discipline had been preserved.

FIONA: That story is a perfect example of your work in many ways, because of how top-down histories always seem to present sailors and pirates as the originators of violence: sailors fight, pirates take ships. Rarely is their experience understood as a category of workers created through violence.

MARCUS: That is crucial. One of the most important things I discovered was that the regime of violence aboard the ship was central to the work experience of sailors and to their reasons for resistance. And it was certainly crucial to the decisions of pirates to set up alternative societies in which the cat-o'-nine-tails would not govern.

Another thing I had to find out was how people came to be sailors. This led me into the history of enclosure, dispossession, and expropriation, by which people lost land and had nothing to sell but their labour. I thought it sadly poetic that sailors were called "hands," the hands of the ship, for their hands were all they had. They worked for a wage in a big international labour market where the conditions of labour were rough. They were, in some ways, the leading edge of the working class. They had no property and no artisanal skill, and could therefore only sell their bodies for money. Those bodies took a ferocious beating. I read a sailor's petition to the court: he had been beaten so badly that he could no longer go aloft because he got dizzy. I could see how the discipline of class was destroying the bodies of these sailors. Of course, it was no accident that a large proportion of beggars in every port city were former sailors. Some had had an arm blown off or were crippled this way or that. A ship was a dangerous workplace.

FIONA: In that period, what would be the average working life of a maritime worker?

MARCUS: It is hard to say. We don't have good documentation. One thing we do know is that sailors would work for a few years, then leave the sea because it was such harsh labour. If I had to guess, I would say a typical working life at sea would be eight to twelve years. Some survived against the odds. We have a journal of a sailor who worked at sea for forty years. He kept the account of his life in a wax-stopped joint of bamboo. It survived and is now in the National Maritime Museum in Greenwich, England. But that was not typical. As for pirates, most of them were young, in their twenties. Some of them became pirates to live as well and as freely as they could for as long as they could. They did not expect to live long. Living on a pirate ship was something they chose over slavery, as they called it—the violent drudgery of the merchant or the naval ship.

Pirate Ways of Knowing

FIONA: So most pirates would have already experienced the direct violence of the ship as sailors before turning to piracy? Did they not generally go straight into piracy?

MARCUS: Almost all pirates were experienced sailors, and it really was a fraternity of skilled maritime workers.

FIONA: They took the skills they learned on the factory-ship to then create another reality?

MARCUS: The European deep-sea sailing ship was one of the most sophisticated technologies in the world in its day, and piracy showed what might happen when a group of working people took it over. The takeover of ships resembled the factory seizures of the late nineteenth and early twentieth centuries. Sailors, as pirates, seized their workplaces and organized them in new ways. They elected their captain, they changed the system of discipline, and they feasted on food and drink. This was the antithesis of the shipboard life that they had known on merchant or naval vessels. They took control of a powerful machine, which made them dangerous to the powers of the day. One reason why authorities wanted to hang these men was that they used these vessels to create societies that subverted the typical shipboard social order.

FIONA: Dangerous knowledge?

MARCUS: Very dangerous. It wasn't simply that they were attacking property, although that was part of it. They were also showing how a ship could be run in a different way, and this could have damaging effects on other lines of seafaring work. The idea of electing your captain is about as different a practice as one can imagine, because the powers of an eighteenth-century sea captain were nearly absolute.

FIONA: How would that democratic impulse circulate?

MARCUS: Movements from below on land fed it. For example, some pirates had been involved in peasant revolts. Some had been part of urban crowds. Remember, this was a pre-democratic age, so I would emphasize the novelty of electing captains and other officers. The history of democracy owes something to these poor people, who did not have the right to vote anywhere on earth. This is part of what makes their story so dramatic. They were not aristocrats who ran away to sea on a lark. They were poor, working sailors who were engaged in an extraordinary experiment of trying to build a different sort of society. And that, of course, was completely unacceptable to the rulers of the day.

Violent Pedagogies

FIONA: I want to return to the question of violence in your work. Violence and political fear play a contradictory role in that they divide people and then bring them together in new ways. I'm interested in your thoughts on the relevance of this process for understanding fear as a social relation in capitalism.

MARCUS: One of the things that struck me early on was that violence was instrumental to the creation of the world market. This was true in expropriating peasants and turning them into labourers so they could be moved onto ships and plantations, areas where production for the world market was organized. But it was also essential to organize the labour to move the commodities. This violence is no residue of an archaic mode of production. This is highly functional violence, geared to making a ship run and giving its captain the ability to control people. So we find this on merchant ships, on naval ships. Pirates built countercultures on their vessels.

The violence was most extreme on slave ships, which had a dual system of terror. I use the word deliberately, because captains employed terror to control people on the slavers. One part of the dual system was for the sailors, the other for the enslaved. The captain had to manage the two sides carefully. Both groups were governed through violence—although not equivalently, I would emphasize. The violence done to the enslaved was much greater. But in certain instances the enslaved might witness a sailor flogged to death by the captain. The violence may have been more or less identical to what would have been visited upon the leader of an insurrection among the enslaved.

In our book *The Many-Headed Hydra*, Peter Linebaugh and I talk about the varieties of violence. There is the violence of expropriation; the violence of the Middle Passage, when people were being moved from one part of the Atlantic economy to another; and the violence of exploitation of the people who worked on the ships, plantations, and factories. And finally, there was the violence of repression used when people dared to resist the situations in which they found themselves. An interlocking set of violent practices produced fear. These were instrumental to making modern capitalism.

Social life on the ship was a war of nerves. The captain would try to intimidate the crew using violence and the threat of violence, and the crew would sometimes try to counter-intimidate the captain in an effort to limit his power. The resistance didn't always work, but it was always part of the power dynamic on every ship. Pirates, when they set up on their own, frequently saw themselves as avengers of the poor sailors, so when they captured ships, they turned disciplinary violence back onto the ship captain. Fear and the effort to overcome fear were central to social life on slave ships, and indeed, many other vessels.

FIONA: Given this jittery dynamic, did ship captains always see "their" sailors as potential pirates?

MARCUS: Not always. It would depend on the larger situation. After piracy was eradicated in the late 1720s, it would never again exist on an international scale. But I think it would be fair to say that every captain saw almost every sailor as a potential mutineer. That was parallel to every slave owner seeing every slave as a potential rebel. Both depended on violence to maintain control.

FIONA: How do you see us still living with that legacy?

MARCUS: The violence of expropriation worldwide continues unabated. The growth of slum-filled mega-cities is fuelled by expropriation from various rural hinterlands. The violence of the Middle Passage continues as labourers are brought from one place to another. The people who organize the movement of coerced sex workers, for example, depend on violent transportation systems. The violence of exploitation and the violence of repression obviously continue. In a real way, the eighteenth century is the origin of modern capitalism, which has lasted to the present. It has changed over time because of struggles from below. Many of the lineaments of that system are still in place.

FIONA: Many readers have found a surprisingly hopeful sense of political inspiration in these histories of violence that you uncover. Perhaps this is why your studies on the Atlantic revolutionary movement and the radical pirates have found a wide readership among the alter-globalization crowd. You reveal a sense of how the power to dominate and exploit is in actuality rather brittle. From this point of view, we could think about the role of terror as not just terrifying, but also as a response to persistent, rumbling agitation for alternative forms of life. Do you see hope as part of thinking against the enclosures?

MARCUS: I do, and I like the way you put the question. I think the inspiring thing about this history is the way in which people steadfastly and courageously resisted the violence and terror. I think you're absolutely right that this speaks to the fragility of power. The authorities were never entirely clear, in their own minds, if they were in control of this motley crew. The ruthlessness of power on the slave ship suggested that the situation was precarious. The hopeful part of the story is the self-activity from below: the planned and spontaneous things people did to free themselves from exploitation and oppression. We need this history as we think about the future. The weight of the violence from above is great, and it would be easy to be discouraged by it. But if you study the history from below, you'll see that the violence was always contested. People did not accept the circumstances in which they found themselves. They fought back, even in the extreme circumstances of the slave ship.

Exemplary Punishment, Refusal of Fear

FIONA: Did the early modern motley crew see fear and terror as something to overtly challenge?

MARCUS: Yes, because in the eighteenth century all punishments were meant to be exemplary. Public hangings, for instance, were big spectacles meant to teach lessons about private property, about power, class, staying in one's place. The same was true onboard a ship, especially a slave ship, where a captain would pick out a "troublemaker" among the crew or among the enslaved, then use him or her as a medium through which to enact power through violence. The captain multiplied the power by calling everyone up on deck to make them witness its gruesome, bloody effects. In the Royal Navy, when mutineers were flogged, frequently to death, the admiral would sometimes bring the entire fleet together around the spectacle. He wanted to multiply the social visibility of the violence and to use fear to govern the motley crew.

A special and revealing theatre of fear was acted out at the gallows. Those many who attended public hangings drew on a long and powerful tradition of cursing the authorities, of "dying game," refusing to give in, declining to show fear. Pirates faced execution before big crowds, which usually included the richest people of the colony. In Virginia in 1720, condemned pirates were given a glass of wine before their execution, and one of them stepped forward to toast "damnation to the governor and confusion to the colony." Some would probably come to watch the condemned curse the powerful as part of the drama. The people facing death demonstrated power by refusing to show penitence and deference. Some did what the authorities wanted them to do, like pray, partly because they hoped to get a reprieve, which did occasionally happen. The king might extend the royal hand of mercy to a man with a rope around his neck. In any case, the gallows was a stage for fearlessness, where people said, "Even in death, we are not afraid of you."

FIONA: People would come to watch not necessarily out of a sadistic impulse or as an act of education, as the authorities believed, but out of solidarity?

MARCUS: It would depend on the time and place, and I'm sure every crowd assembled to watch a hanging contained within it people of various motivations. Some sought titillation, while others wanted to see the solemn authority of the law imposed. But for a substantial number, especially poor people, the intent was different. They turned up to show solidarity with the people who were going to be hanged. I found an instance, in Jamaica in 1717, when a mob rescued a gang of pirates from the gallows. They seized them and carried them away in triumph! This kind of thing didn't happen often, because there were often armed guards present at executions, but the resistance of the crowd was part of the social dynamics surrounding the gallows.

FIONA: What do you mean when you use the expression "the right to escape" in your writing?

MARCUS: We see among sailors and other workers a struggle for autonomous mobility. Rulers contrived all kinds of extraordinary measures to keep sailors on the ship, slaves on the plantation, and workers in the factory. But in all three settings, workers continued to escape: as deserters, in the case of sailors; as runaway slaves who would form Maroon communities [resistant communities established by escaped slaves in the Caribbean]; and as workers who would slip away and go to the next factory town to find a better situation. This is the self-granted right of escape. It is a powerful form of resistance that is sometimes wrongly considered as individualistic. In seafaring, there existed a tradition of desertion, of sailors escaping in groups. When the accumulation of capital requires workers to be in a specific place, the struggle over movement is a real assertion of will and power. The point is crucial to labour history. In fact, I wrote an essay years ago called "Good Hands, Stout Hearts and Fast Feet: The History of Working People in Early America,"* which was about the sharp clash over workers' right to mobility in labour-scarce colonies.

---

* *Labour/Le Travail* 10 (Autumn 1982): 123–144.

FIONA: This struggle for autonomous mobility seems inextricable from the original enclosures of the commons. Here we had an enormous dispossession, which forced masses of people to go on the move, and they then needed, from the perspective of the owning classes and the state, to be controlled, contained, and put to work.

MARCUS: The issue of movement is two sided, because when people are expropriated, they are forced to move. This is what happened in sixteenth- and seventeenth-century England during the enclosures: "masterless men and women," swept from the feudal estates, escaped the dominant means of social control. Society seemed to be coming apart at the seams; vagabonds symbolized the process. Set in motion by enclosures, they would eventually be re-enclosed in new spaces of work. That might be on the docks, in the fields as agricultural labourers, in the army, the navy, merchant shipping, or manufacturing. English imperialist Richard Hakluyt saw overseas colonies as "prisons without walls" for rebellious home spirits.

Accumulating Bodies

FIONA: The poorhouse.

MARCUS: Or the poorhouse. The authorities tried to enclose former workers, who sought to move from place to place to keep body and soul together. Sailors provide an interesting example of mobility because they had to move around as a condition of their work. Their movement was required to make the system work. But they translated that functional mobility into something subversive—the freedom to jump ship, change captains, or find a better wage: in short, the freedom to use mobility for their own purposes, not the owner's purposes. Again we see the two-sidedness. This is where new mechanisms of social control, including the prison, become important. Expropriation unleashed a tremendous chaos, which the ruling class now had to manage through new institutions.

FIONA: The law?

MARCUS: Law is crucial to the rise of private property. A big question was, and is, now that people have been expropriated, how are they going to live?

Here the so-called "criminal justice system" comes into play. A lot of the historical evidence I found about working people in the early modern era came from court records about people who were being disciplined by the courts for their unruliness. Many were desperately helping themselves to various kinds of subsistence, and were therefore breaking the law.

In 2007 we had 2.2 million people incarcerated in the United States. People for whom the capitalist system no longer has use are contained in huge holding pens. An accumulation of bodies is always part of what Karl Marx called the "primitive accumulation of capital."

FIONA: Do you think that is the result of capital's efforts to escape workers?

MARCUS: The flight of capital is a major issue of modern world history. Capitalists will always try to escape those areas where workers have waged successful struggles, where wages are high and benefits substantial. They will always search for cheaper, more manageable sources of labour. The issue of the autonomous mobility of labour is the ghostly shadow of the mobility of capital.

FIONA: I want to ask you about your interest in language and poetry. You use a lot of poetry, and your writing style is poetic. And poetry was central to popular culture in the times you write about. What do you think about the role of language—the creation of new languages and terms like the ones that appear in your books: motley crew, hydrarchy, shipmate, outcasts of all nations, the many-headed hydra? These phrases seem to exemplify new modes of being in the world, new resistant activities.

MARCUS: There is poetry in people's struggle. It is important for us to see what people are trying to do for themselves, often under harsh, difficult, even deadly circumstances. There is a beauty in resistance; forgetting that is part of our defeat. If we remember it, we can hopefully feel some connection to, and take power from, those who have gone before. People learn history as they make history, wrote C.L.R. James.

As for these phrases you mentioned, in writing *The Many-Headed Hydra*, Peter Linebaugh and I were keen to understand reality through the concepts and language of the time. So we paid careful attention when people from either above or below described a collectivity, especially a collectivity taking action—more specifically a collectivity taking radical action. Those terms—motley crew, hydrarchy, and so forth—were constituent parts of a language of class.

FIONA: The collectivities you urge us to remember are not necessarily organizations?

MARCUS: Not necessarily. It could be a mob that formed at a moment's notice because of a food shortage or an arrest. You could say the mob is a form of organization, because it does have a tradition and in some places it is an institution. But it comes and goes; its life is fitful, circumstantial. It is a fugitive sort of organization, like many working-class collectivities. It arises in situations of need, and it disappears.

Peter and I also wanted to show how those massive collectivities known as race, class, and the nation arose in the late eighteenth century. We decided it was necessary to go back and write history from below before notions of race, class, and nation had formed and hardened. And we found all kinds of cooperation across those socially constructed lines of power, to suggest liberating possibilities. There was a time when people thought differently about what they often called "the human race," which was not divided by the categories that seem so crucial in our time.

FIONA: You also explore the radical use of the term "human race."

MARCUS: Radicals used the term in the eighteenth century as an anti-racializing strategy. They said, "We are the human race, we are alike, we are one, we are united. We are not black and white. We are not your chopped-up categories. We are together. We have common rights, common purposes, common humanity." We thought of this as a kind of "Enlightenment from below." There was an embrace of differences, rather than willed division based on them.

One of the great challenges of our time is to come up with unifying ideas. Many people are working on progressive causes, but they don't feel that they are part of something larger. They don't feel that they are part of a movement that can change the world. They want to change one part of it—labour, environment, women's issues—and this work is crucial. But big, important, radical change happens when people feel that lots of people are working together and that what they want in the end is something similar—another way of being and living. I think that we can make those connections, build new kinds of movements.

Laughing at Fear

FIONA: Do you think that radical pirates saw themselves as politically marginal, as many historians do?

MARCUS: I think they saw themselves as actors on a world stage. Lots of rebels have seen themselves that way. It is interesting that people often see the meanings of their own lives in terms of big historical processes. Pirates were called the "villains of all nations." That is a big, international proposition. And they were indeed made up of all nations. They were out there on the seas enacting dramas of global interest, and I do think they were often conscious of this. They became international outlaws, and they gloried in their badness. They said, "Yes, we're pirates. We are your greatest nightmares." They combined humour and defiance.

I would add that movements from below have frequently demonstrated good humour. Gallows humour is a good example of being able to stare death in the eye and laugh. That takes extraordinary courage. Pirates joked frequently about their own looming executions. This too is a lesson.

FIONA: Speaking of strange ironies, I am curious to know the story of the Jolly Roger. What is this famous flag's background?

MARCUS: Pirates adorned a black flag with symbols of death: a skull and crossbones, or, more commonly, an entire skeleton, which was often holding a knife, a sword, a dart, or an hourglass. Frequently the weapon strikes a heart, from which drops of blood drip down. Pirate flags were therefore more complex than many would have us believe. Their detail emerged from skill: sailors knew how to use needle and thread because they constantly sewed canvas sails to repair them.

The black flag had two basic meanings. One was straightforward and unmistakable. The pirate ship approached a potential prize vessel, raised the Jolly Roger, and sent a clear message: surrender or die. The symbolism worked. When the Jolly Roger went up, the men on the prize vessel almost always surrendered, deciding that it was better to give up than to fight back and perhaps anger the pirates, who were going to capture you sooner or later anyway. They had faster ships, better arms, and more men.

A second set of meanings associated with the Jolly Roger grew from the labour history of the sailors who became pirates. The flag represents a commentary on the lives common sailors were forced to lead. The symbolic skull and crossbones originated among merchant captains, who drew it in the ship's log to record the death of a sailor. Pirates used the same symbol to make an ironic commentary: "We're trapped in a deadly employment, so we'll take this symbol of death and put it on our flag. We will fight under it and we will find life under it. We will live differently, in a new kind of society of our own making."

The other symbols fit the same pattern because the weapons, the striking of the heart, the hourglass, death, violence, and limited time were all part of the experience of the common sailor, who felt that he could escape that world only by becoming a pirate. The embrace of piracy was an affirmative choice, not an act of desperation. The flag thus illuminates the life of the common sailor who would choose to become a pirate.

Another layer of symbolism was religious, or, more precisely, irreligious. Roger was a name for the devil, so a Jolly Roger was a happy, carefree devil. Pirates loved to invert traditional authority: "Afraid of the devil, are you? Okay, we're the devil, then." Blackbeard (Edward Teach) was cunning in the use of such symbolism, playing with satanic imagery. Yet another meaning was sexual, for Roger was a cant word (from the London "criminal" underground) for penis. To roger was to fuck. The black flag also conveyed the message, "Fuck you." The Jolly Roger says a lot about who pirates were.

Pirates also used a blood-red flag, which was a traditional naval symbol: a ship would run up a red flag to indicate that they would not surrender, nor would they accept the surrender of the other side. A red flag indicated that this would be a battle to the death. This is the original meaning of the red flag at sea. In the Liverpool sailors' strike of 1775, which I wrote about in *The Slave Ship*, sailors marched to City Hall under the red flag. Later, in the early nineteenth century, the red flag became a symbol of the European workers' movement. Most people don't know its maritime origins among sailors and pirates.

FIONA: So in a way the flag, the way it's used, is a way of laughing at fear?

MARCUS: Yes, laughing at fear, laughing at death.

FIONA: It sounds like yet another example of a popular symbolic inversion of the kind of violent experience that produced the sailor.

MARCUS: Movements from below can teach us much if we dig into the archives and figure out what people were trying to do, what they were trying to say. Pirates were rebels first and foremost, and this is why we still love them today. Even though much of the history has been lost, and much more of it falsified by Hollywood, we know that pirates were outlaws and we adore them for it. They gathered up all their courage and dared to live beyond the boundaries of the law.

FIONA: This attraction is pretty extraordinary when you think of the amount of effort that was put into demonizing them—the public executions and so on.

MARCUS: Absolutely! Hundreds of pirates were hanged. The rulers won. They eradicated piracy as an international phenomenon. But today, three hundred years later, we don't remember the rulers; we celebrate the pirates. The freebooters have captured the popular imagination. This is why people of all ages are fascinated by pirates. In this way, the outlaws beat the odds. They laughed at the authorities on the gallows, and they would be laughing today if they knew that they were remembered and celebrated while the authorities were not.

Reflections on the Violence of Abstraction

FIONA: How do you think these stories and struggles relate to one of the most significant anti-fear movements, which you have also been closely involved with: the struggle against the death penalty in the US?

MARCUS: I should have said in answer to your first question that another formative experience for me was going into prisons to visit people on death row, especially Mumia Abu-Jamal. The dialectics of fear and terror are obviously central to the movement against the death penalty. Just going into that place, this prison—State Correctional Institution–Greene County, it's called, or SCI-Greene—where most of the death row inmates in Pennsylvania are housed, one confronts the full, deadly force of state power. Some people in that facility have dates to die. Death warrants are acts of terror. It is claimed that the terror "deters" crime, but we know that it does no such thing. On the contrary, it sends the strong message that violence is the means to solve problems.

FIONA: So it is the continuation of exemplary violence, but without the—

MARCUS: Without the crowd. Right. If people who support capital punishment had the courage of their convictions, they would press for public executions. If they were successful, and public executions were to come back, capital punishment would be abolished immediately. Once the violence of execution was no longer abstract to people, they wouldn't tolerate it. The same was true of the slave ship. Once the public knew what really happened on those vessels, once the horrific reality of slave ships was made concrete, abolition of the slave trade followed quickly. The same would be true of capital punishment. Its continuation depends on thinking that somehow it is not happening to real people. Execution is an abstraction. People are not prepared to think about botched executions, which happen again and again and again. Here's a lesson for movements from below: we need to make real to people what any given oppressive situation is actually like.

When I give talks on the death penalty, I often describe what it's like to go into the prison and visit someone on death row: the clang of the steel doors, the tiny visitation cubicle with Plexiglas between you and the person in handcuffs and leg restraints on the other side. I try to make it real and vivid, something that people can imagine and think about. I used to talk with Mumia about this, and he said that in writing his book, *Live from Death Row*, he wondered how much of the reality behind bars people could bear. I had the same question about the slave ship. How much of this reality can people take? But in both cases, the effort to depict a deadly reality was part of the politics of the writing.

FIONA: The prison in Guantanamo Bay is an extension of this strange, violent abstraction. Most of us can't see it and don't have access to it, but we all know that it's part of the same archipelago of events and spaces of power. What do you think the shift towards making it more invisible is about? Is that because of the success of the abolitionist movement?

MARCUS: I think it's partly the success of movements. It's partly what you describe as the vulnerability of power. People are afraid that their actions may have unintended consequences.

FIONA: Like people standing up and saying no?

MARCUS: Yes. If the American public had any idea of how executions are botched, they would probably abolish it. It's all done secretly. If people had any idea about the real conditions at Guantanamo, the policy would probably be changed. People in power have a desire and need to disguise what they do, and prisons exemplify that. But it is also the case that certain limitations have been placed on them by popular movements. They are not free to do everything they want.

We had an interesting situation a few years ago, when Mumia was involved in a hunger strike, and we managed to get the direct number of the prison warden out to lots of people in the community. Many called in protest. One woman actually got through. She must have been a sympathetic soul, because the warden actually had quite a long conversation with her. He said, "Do you have any idea how hard it is having a famous inmate like Mumia Abu-Jamal in your prison? Do you know that his supporters will burn up a fax machine if I threaten to cut his dreadlocks?" He was complaining to this woman about how hard his life as a warden was! The movement made him feel embattled. And I'll tell you, prison wardens are not a species that thrive in the light of day. They prefer to live under a dark rock, out of the glare of public scrutiny.

This story suggests that social movements often have more power than they know. Shining a light into a dark space becomes a big part of what we must do—to let people know how power works. We have seen slow but important incremental changes to the death penalty. One justice called it "tinkering with the machinery of death," which I think is a good way to put it. What we really need to do is abolish it once and for all. I think we will.

FIONA: Because it's untenable?

MARCUS: Because the whole criminal justice system is just so patently unfair. When I speak to groups about this, I often begin with a question: "Based on your experience and your experience only, I want you to tell me what you would do if you were in this situation. Let's assume you've been charged with capital murder and you're facing the death penalty. In that situation, would you rather be rich and guilty, or poor and innocent?" I once asked this question in a large Sunday school class in Pittsburgh, presided over by one of the leading black judges in the city. I did not know how he would respond to this. But when I posed the question "rich and guilty or poor and innocent?" the judge bellowed out, "Rich and guilty! Rich and guilty! Believe me, I know how the system works!" Here's the trick: anyone who answers the question "rich and guilty" must support the abolition of the death penalty. Because if it is true that the poor and innocent are more likely to be executed, then the system is completely corrupt. It follows that we must not allow people to die under these circumstances.

2

SILVIA FEDERICI

Remembering Resistance from the Witch Hunts to Alter-Globalization

S ILVIA FEDERICI is a feminist activist and scholar whose writing and political activities have contributed enormously to the broad Autonomist tradition. Known for her intellectual generosity, sharp, nonconformist thought, and searing critiques of capitalist society, Federici's work has inspired the generation of social activists associated with the rise of the alter-globalization movement. Her own political roots were formed in the Marxist radical left of the women's movement, and she was one of the principal figures associated with the Wages for Housework movement, which in the 1970s and 1980s opened up a crucial and highly contentious debate about the role of the labour of reproduction in capitalist accumulation. Since the 1980s, Federici has been producing original and influential feminist critiques of capitalist globalization. In the late 1970s she embarked on a study of the history of women in the transition to capitalism, which turned into an exploration of the early modern witch hunts. Her widely read and much-debated book *Caliban and the Witch: Women, the Body and Primitive Accumulation* (Autonomedia, 2004) presents a revisionist global history of the devastation wrought by the systematic mass killings of women in early modern Europe and its colonies. In our own era, aggressive capitalist globalization has been accompanied by a rise in targeted killings of women and girls—a phenomenon common enough to have its own term, *femicide*. Given its prescience, it is unsurprising that the book has circulated around the world, inspiring a new generation of lively discussion about the role of feminist practice amid the global crisis.

Born in Italy in the midst of the Second World War, Federici moved to the United States in the late 1960s armed with a scholarship to study philosophy. She soon became involved in student activism and the blossoming women's liberation movement. In the mid-1980s, Federici moved to Nigeria to take up a contract teaching position at the University of Port Harcourt, and there she witnessed firsthand the social devastation wrought by World Bank and International Monetary Fund austerity programs that were at that time being savagely imposed on "debtor nations." But alongside the social destruction, she also discovered thriving practices of commoning, as people sought to secure and develop their access to a livelihood outside of the encroaching dominance of the capitalist market in both the city and the countryside. Out of this experience, Federici became an early theorist of the enduring relevance of the commons in the face of contemporary processes of neoliberal enclosure. In this discussion, Federici weaves together her reflections on growing up under the shadow of fascism in Italy, the contemporary significance of the early modern witch hunts on the social and economic order, and ongoing struggles for the reconstruction of the commons in the period of global capitalist structural adjustment.

Fear Needn't Paralyze You

FIONA: First, will you tell me about your background? How do you think the question of the politics of fear matters to your work and thought?

SILVIA: I was a small child growing up in Italy during the Second World War. Movements in World War II against fascism, racism, and Nazism were formative to my understanding of politics, movement building, and solidarity. Whatever the movement was, the question of organization, the question of building networks, was central. Ultimately the power of movements allowed people in them to overcome their fear of being part of a struggle. They formed a collective identity, a history that went beyond them. This meant that the always-looming possibility of their destruction was not devastating or paralyzing in the way that one may think it would be. In a sense, even the sacrifice of life would not be the end of their individual history, either, because in that struggle against fascism people were part of a collective self. They were part of something that transcended the temporal limits of their lives and that made death, the ever-present possibility of death, bearable.

You know those slogans that sound rather rhetorical, like "You can kill me but you won't destroy the struggle"? They actually have a very profound meaning. In the dangerous and scary struggle against fascism and Nazism, people became part of a broader body. When you join such a struggle, you become part of something that projects you way beyond your own lifespan. The destruction of your own individual body means something different then. You build for the future. You identify with the destiny of the new generation. And that is what gives people strength. Ultimately it makes you overcome the fear of pain or dying, and gives you the confidence that your death is not going to be in vain.

FIONA: So it is not necessarily a matter of having no fear. When I imagine the anonymous anti-fascist struggles that took place all over Italy and throughout Europe, in small villages as well as in cities, I think of how risky and scary it must have been for people when any kind of protection could only come from the community and the movement. It is hard to imagine vanquishing fear while fighting fascism. Certainly the strategy of fear used by fascists sought to paralyze people. Besides scapegoating, which is, of course, a fascist specialty, making people feel helpless and alone seems to be one of the most effective ways that fear is used politically.

SILVIA: Yes. You don't overcome the fear, but you don't let it paralyze you. It is impossible to overcome fear. If you are involved in the struggle for justice, even if you don't fear for your own life, you fear for the people around you. You fear for the lives of your friends. Every time you engage in an initiative or action, it is not only yourself who is involved. So you can't overcome fear, but you can begin by organizing around the forces that are opposing you, and by deepening the sense of the struggle. This ability to build a collective history is ultimately what gives you strength.

FIONA: Individualizing or privatizing people's fears—fears of economic ruin, social irrelevance, or what have you—seems to be an effective strategy for making people feel alone and helpless.

SILVIA: In the 1940s, those in the resistance against the fascists or the Nazis had a very strong moment of collective identification and organization. The difference today is, perhaps, that what people are up against is more blurred. What is also more blurred, what is harder to identify, is what constitutes the community of resistance. In today's social struggles against our world's manifold injustices, who is there with you? It is hard to know. Who can you really count on? This is happening for a broad variety of reasons, but I think it is helpful to look at the kind of community that existed up until the 1940s and 1950s, when people shared a long history together. You studied together. You went to the same elementary school. You knew each other's parents, brothers, and sisters. You shared so many moments of your life. You knew what kind of people they were. There was a kind of trust or mistrust that you could have that was based on life experiences shared together. You grew up together. Whereas today, think of a place like New York City. You meet people about whose life you know nothing. You may meet them in a meeting or at a demonstration. But in a profound sense, in many cases they are strangers to you. You don't know what you can count upon.

That type of very tightly knit community, where people identify on the basis of their class history, is less and less available today. You do see these incredible struggles taking place in villages in Mexico, but that is coming from communities that are very tightly knit. People know who is going to be there tomorrow—who is going to spring into action tomorrow if you are picked up by police, or when you go on strike. For example, when teachers went on strike in Oaxaca in 2006, all of a sudden a flood of people came out to support them, because those communities had a history together. The teachers had taken care of the kids in the villages when the parents had gone picking coffee in Guatemala. They had taken care of the kids in terms of their everyday life, not just teaching. In many urban environments, in the US and around the world, the social fabric has broken down. This doesn't mean that the social fabric can't be woven back together in a process of struggle. But as a starting point, it makes it far more difficult to create a sense of strength that enables you to confront the possibility of repression. And today, political repression is articulated on so many different levels that it is far more difficult to know what you are up against.

There is a science of repression that has been developed, particularly in the US, devoted to figuring out how to disaggregate people as a way to control them. So you have to divide people up: you have those who are going to be shot, and those who are going to get a visit from the FBI and be given a warning, maybe a few days in jail. Or you have those whose phones will be tapped. So there is a great diversification of the means of repression. And this makes it far more difficult to see the face of what you're up against—to measure the actual danger you face.

Let's return to Italy in the 1940s for a moment and the example of the partisans. I use this example because I come from a part of Italy that was heavily partisan, and I grew up hearing their stories. Some of the partisans were fifteen, sixteen years old. They were running all over the hills, keeping the different commandants of the different partisan groups in contact. They were kids! And they knew very well that if they were captured by the fascists, or by the Nazis once Italy was occupied, not only would they be killed, but most likely they would die under torture. They had a pretty clear idea of what the relations of forces were, what their chances were, and what would happen to them if they were caught. There are still many places in the world where the lines are very clear, where in a very real sense you know what awaits you if you engage in political struggle. But the situation today in places like the US and Europe is far more blurred, because the confrontation is not as sharp and the means of repression are much more indirect. That doesn't mean repression no longer exists. It is articulated in different ways for different groups: if you're an immigrant, a black adult, a black youth, or a white middle-class person, the experience is sharply different.

The question of fear is created by the general sense of uncertainty. Often now there is a level of self-censorship. Perhaps this is because the situation is not always clear in terms of what is happening and in terms of understanding who is there with you. There certainly is a strong understanding that there is general repression, but its shape and foundation are not always clear. You can't necessarily grasp its concreteness.

Movement, Solidarity, and Love

FIONA: Historically, confusion has indeed been decisive to sowing political fear. The history of repression appears to be filled with strategies of deliberate confusion, such as when some dissidents are killed while others are not. Political dissidents end up devoting enormous amounts of energy to wondering, "Why did they target that person and not me, when I am involved in the same kind of work organizing a union or a social justice project in my neighbourhood?" and so on. Deliberate confusion seems to be an efficient way to weave fear and distrust into the social fabric.

SILVIA: It is difficult to speak about this on a general level. If you're a Tamil in Sri Lanka, the situation is very clear. There are hundreds of situations like that around the world. The situation I've described with the anti-fascist partisans is everywhere today. I need to use a point of reference, so I'm going to use New York, because we're here. I think what I'm trying to say is that if today we're talking about the alter-globalization movement in the US, it is very difficult for people to really calibrate what they're risking. And in such a context, people begin a process of self-censorship. I think self-censorship and the paralyzing effects of fear have to do with the two factors I've been talking about: the uncertainty about who is with you, and the uncertainty about what is at stake in your struggle. If something is a fundamental issue in my life, then I am willing to take all kinds of risks. But if I'm not clear on whether what I'm fighting for is ultimately extremely important, even if it doesn't immediately succeed, then the risks would appear more frightening. So the question of the nature of the community that you're coming from and the nature of the struggle you are engaged in—the question of what it is about and what is at stake (and understanding what you're really up against)—takes on a great deal of personal and political importance. What will be the effect? What will be the response? What are the risks that you're running? When we talk about self-reproducing movements, we talk about not dividing the personal and the political. When we talk about a community that is sharing not only the struggle but also a whole life, you cannot really have a separate life and just show up for the demonstrations. If you do, you'll have no idea about the person next to you. Are they going to help you if you get clubbed? But the sense of community is not just about whether people will be there to defend you. It is also a question of your own investment: you take risks for other people that you may not even take for yourself. There is a question of solidarity and love. People give their lives, which they might not give if only their own existence were at stake. But solidarity and love take you beyond yourself—always. They are the greatest forces in every struggle.

Intimate Resistance

FIONA: If we can go back again to the first question, one thing that stands out in your thinking, writing, and political activism has been your deep understanding of the intimate dimensions of resistance. What is it in your own history that shaped your particular approach to thinking and acting in the world?

SILVIA: So many things! As for many of my generation, I think the most fundamental influence was World War II. I was born in the last year of the war, but it was always present in my life. It was a central theme in my family and in my community. The war communicated a number of messages. The first was a message about politics, about history. It forced fundamental questions about what a political life is. It made clear that there are enormous injustices and divisions in the world, which in turn brought the importance of resistance and sacrifice to the forefront, and the idea that certain atrocities should never happen again. So very early on, the question of injustice and struggling against injustice was central and continuously repeated. In a way, I grew up with a double message: that the world had gone terribly wrong and that this was not a world of happiness and ease, but at the same time, it was a world in which it was possible to resist, and many people did. So it was a world where you were expected to struggle against injustice. And of course, at the same time, there was a great suspicion of authority and the state. The experience of fascism showed that you couldn't trust the state, you couldn't trust the authorities. So that was definitely an important influence. The war affected everyone I knew.

A second influence, less directly present, was the anti-colonial movement. It was not a direct, immediate presence when I was growing up—it came to us in school, through adults, and in newspapers—but there was a sense that out there was a world in revolt, a world on the move, in a process of broad change. There was a sense that this was not a world that was settled, by any measure. My youth was filled with news of change in Kenya, France, or Algeria.

Another major factor was coming to the US in the 1960s, and my experience of the student movement and the women's movement. The women's movement was the culmination of a whole set of questions that had been building in my personal life and in the world. My sense of unease with the world found a name in the women's movement. I recognized right away that the women's movement gave a name to many of the questions and problems that I felt in my life. It became a politics and an analysis. It enabled me to grasp the narrow-mindedness of my father or my teachers, for example. This was a turning point that expanded my consciousness.

Each of these influences raised different problems and possibilities. But fundamentally, they showed that this world was changing. And I've seen tremendous change in my own lifetime that I never would have thought possible—the kind of transformations I see now in women's lives, even though they are a far cry from liberation: the kind of life that many women can have, where they have a certain amount of control to decide about the children they have, or marriage, or their sexual life. It is really fantastic. I never, never imagined this would be possible during my lifetime. To be able to have a life with a certain degree of autonomy was certainly not the situation of our mothers. And this is certainly not the situation of women on a broad, world level. But the number of women that can actually have that experience has increased. And that was certainly not the case in the world in which I came of age, and not for my mother or the other women around me. Because I was an early feminist, the circumstances of women were a battle when I was a teenager. My father used to laugh at the idea of women bus drivers. Every time I see a woman bus driver now, it seems almost incredible that he could be so narrow-minded. And he was an intellectual, he was a philosopher! Even though my father encouraged me to read, to write, to discuss politics, the idea that a woman's role was domestic was firmly entrenched. This was the context of the Italy in which I grew up.

A Political Life in Motion

FIONA: In the mid-1980s, Reagan was in power in the US, political repression intensified in Italy, and you went to teach philosophy at a university in Nigeria, which was also soon to be in the throes of its own political crisis triggered by austerity measures imposed by the World Bank and the IMF. You have written and spoken with great anguish about the neoliberal attacks on public education and people's lives more generally during this era of brutal austerity, imposed across most of the African continent. Tell me about your move to Nigeria in the 1980s. What brought you there, and how did living and working in Africa affect your political thinking?

SILVIA: Africa was important from many different points of view. I always wanted to travel the world; I have always been enormously curious about the world. I went to Nigeria from the US in the early 1980s, at the moment Reagan came to power. The political project in which I'd been involved, Wages for Housework, was ending. I had worked to form another feminist group, one that lasted for a couple of years—we produced a journal called *Tap Dance*. But it became very clear that the times were changing and the spaces that we had opened were closing. Time, energy, and money were getting scarce. And the political climate was suffocating; our efforts were not leading anywhere. So I made a decision to leave the US and take this moment to explore what was happening in other places.

That opened everything up for me. In a sense, I was born again on so many levels, certainly on my level of knowledge—about the "Third World," colonialism, Africa. Many of the issues that I had been reading about in books started to become very real. I developed an understanding that would not have been possible if I had not been there. Also, we arrived in Nigeria at a very important time, a time when the oil boom had turned into an oil bust and the external debt was becoming unmanageable. This prompted discussions about taking loans from the International Monetary Fund. So we arrived at the moment when a huge debate was exploding about the conditions that came with the loan. The whole debate made it very clear that the substance of what was later called "structural adjustment" was in practice a program of recolonization. Whatever attempts at independence from the colonial past people were trying to build were being systematically undermined. Policies were introduced that suffocated local industry and suffocated local trade, and basically opened up regions like Africa to colonial exploitation. In a repeat of the past, the only type of economic activity left was mineral extraction and production for export. There was massive unemployment, and most work could only be found through immigration or at the lowest echelon of the wage scale. I found myself learning again about colonialism and its history, because this is what structural adjustment is about.

In Nigeria, I learned about a society that had a long history of communal relationships. Although colonialism had distorted this history, it still remained. A kind of communalism that had been destroyed in Europe in the fifteenth and sixteenth centuries remained intact in Nigeria when I arrived there. For me, this opened up a whole new understanding about politics. I rediscovered the issue of the commons and struggles around land. In the US, my struggle had been around wages for housework, my thinking still within the framework of the wage relation. The idea behind Wages for Housework was to subvert the division of labour, to subvert the use of unpaid labour in capitalism. But our framework was still the wage, even though we said this challenge to unpaid domestic labour would take us beyond the wage. In Africa I saw that people were fighting not for the wage, but for the land. I'm not sure that this is still true today, since the expropriation has been so profound over the last twenty or twenty-five years. And the imposition of monetary relationships is so strong that now I imagine the question of money is far more prominent. So much effort has gone into making money the gateway to survival, taking away the more direct means of subsistence.

So the question of land became a theme in my own understanding of the world. When I think about a political project for the future, I think about the land. By the land I mean the rivers, the forest, the fruit trees, contact with the natural world, nature as cultural factor, land as spiritual factor, as Native Americans know so well. As Marx said, the land is our inorganic body. It is our first terrain of exchange with the world, of communication with the forces surrounding us. In that way, I think of my time in Nigeria, where land struggles are indivisible from politics, as a third major development.

Terrorizing Women

FIONA: Let's turn to a major theme running through your work and political practice: the story of the witch hunts. You have written extensively about how the misogynist violence behind the witch hunts was a form of political violence. In our own period of capitalist expansion, we have witnessed a surge in extreme violence against women. This violence is global in scope, but it is concentrated in specific sites that are also places of intense capitalist exploitation, such as Ciudad Juarez and the Democratic Republic of the Congo. While this violence is typically explained in decontextualized cultural terms, your work lays out instead a political critique of it. What does the story of the early modern witch hunts tell us about the political nature of violence against women?

SILVIA: Yes, it is political violence. Unfortunately the witch hunts have returned in parts of the world. That violence against women is political, because it is always perpetrated in relation to the kind of functions or roles that women are expected to play. The violence is instrumental to enforcing those functions. Even today, one of the main reasons women are subjected to violence by men has to do with questions of housework, being available for sex, or the whole issue of dependency of the woman on the man. The violence is political because it is a violence that men have been allowed to carry out and it has been somewhat legitimized, even if there are more laws against it now. But in the history of capitalism, violence against women has been legitimized because, in a way, it has been a central part of the regulation of women's labour, a way of forcing women to perform in a certain way, to provide a certain type of work, particularly because this work is unpaid. The less money-wages men have had available to mediate the exchange with women, the wages in exchange for her work, the more they resorted to violence. In fact, you can look at rape that way, the kind of violence that forces women to provide sexual services without giving any payment to her. It is political because this violence has been condoned by the state, it has a legitimacy, and it has been part of the sexual and social division of labour, of unpaid services provided to men in exchange for economic support. Violence has been the mechanism that has ensured the functioning of that relation.

FIONA: When you see this kind of violence returning and spiking in certain places, what do you think? Today, patterns of misogynist, murderous violence are often referred to as a femicide, or gendered genocide. Is there a way of thinking about the innumerable cases of femicide in a way that could help explain the phenomenon? Can we analyze it in general political terms?

SILVIA: I think it's true that this violence has taken on new dimensions over the last twenty years. What I'm presenting now is the general setup in terms of the functioning of gender relationships to the organization of work and accumulation. But I think in recent years there has been an enormous escalation of violence. Not only quantitatively, but I do think there is evidence that there is more violence against women. Violence has been growing in the last two or three decades. And I think there are several causes for this.

One is that more and more women have been resisting the mandate to provide free services for men. Women have been resisting dependency on men by expanding their areas of autonomy, of independence. If you take a second job, you reduce the work you do in the home. You decide not to marry. You have only temporary relationships with men, have a child alone, have relationships with other women. Certainly the emotional investment that women have put into men and into housework has diminished incredibly. And this has been a source of tremendous anger. And of course, another dimension is male fear of competition with women for jobs, because women are paid less. But fundamentally, men see women escaping their control.

I think there is another dimension to this violence, which is very important. It can be understood as a response to structural adjustment, the economic attack on the male wage that has taken place internationally over the last three decades, and capital's attack on people's access to the means of subsistence. One of the responses has been to use not only women's labour but also women's bodies as a means of exchange, so that men who do not have a wage are not able to set up a family. But what they do is use women's labour, women's bodies, as means of exchange. We can see this, for example, in some of the different forms of prostitution that have emerged in this context. But that creates a whole level of violence on its own. It is an extension of that violence that men used to engage in by forcing women to do the housework.

We can also see this in dowry murders, where a man murders his wife so he can remarry and get a second dowry. So there's been an epidemic, particularly among lower-middle-class men, who kill their wives so they can gain a second dowry. They see the woman as a means of personal accumulation. Or think of the witch hunts that are taking place today in parts of Africa. In many cases, these witch hunts are being instigated from above. This is very important to understand. Local chiefs and power figures, in complicity with foreign companies, try to sell the communal lands to mining ventures and so forth. They use the charge of witchcraft as a way of dividing the community and expropriating people from their lands. But there is also a part of those witch hunts that actually comes from within the communities themselves, or from men in the families of the victims. The women accused are often older women, living alone, holding on to a piece of land, not wanting to give it up or pass it on to the next generation. They are the targets. And this is true in many regions. In Tanzania, it is calculated that every year more than a thousand older women die this way. It is happening in India and in Nepal, too. There is growing evidence that older women who have a little bit of land, or access to communal land, are now in danger of being accused of witchcraft, then expelled from their villages or murdered.

I see this as part of a whole devaluation of women's labour. The old woman who no longer represents an asset is a target. She cannot provide sex, she cannot provide children. She cannot be prostituted. And she is seen as an obstacle. Her presence in the community is not valued. And this is becoming more prominent now because of the extension of the monetary relationship. That extension I was referring to before in our discussion about structural adjustment is having a specific impact on women, especially older women, who have been engaged in subsistence farming, and who are increasingly seen as nonproductive. Women are more and more devalued because they do not provide access to the world of commodities, which is becoming more and more extensive. Nor do they provide access to the world of monetary relationships, which is more and more becoming a condition for survival.

I see two fundamental motives at work in this violence against women. They are tightly related, and whichever is predominant depends very much on the context. One is the devaluation of women's lives, labour, and bodies in capitalism. This devaluation is functional to the fact that women are destined to become unpaid workers. Second is the need to force women to perform certain types of work. So the question turns on the labour that women are expected to perform and the low value that is placed on that labour, and on their lives in general. I think violence against women is political because fundamentally there has been a struggle around it, and in a sense, the state has been forced to change its relationship with women. The women's movement has forced this change, which has led to new legislation. The whole campaign by the United Nations on behalf of women is an example of that.

FIONA: How do you see the role of the state?

SILVIA: The state has attempted to create a direct relationship with women. In the old regime, the state did not have a direct relationship with women. Its relationship with women was mediated by men, and this relationship stopped working because the women's struggle threw it into a crisis. So in a sense, the state has tried to create a more direct relationship, and this was certainly one outcome. Women have gained more autonomy from men, and in that process they have gained a more direct relationship to capital and to the state; there is no question about it. Today, women confront capital more directly than when so many were working primarily in the home. At that time, they confronted capital and the state indirectly, through men, through the male wage, and through the production of labour power. Women still do this, of course. It has not disappeared. And there is a question of how much this dynamic has actually been reduced. But the reality is that women are present in waged work and have a direct relationship to capital and the state that they did not have before. At the same time, women are fundamentally the main subject of the reproduction of the workforce, whether it is in a socialized form or at home and unwaged.

So there is the ambiguity of women juggling the two roles. The law still reflects that contradiction. We see this in its more expansive and vicious attacks against women, in the continuous chipping away at women's right to control their bodies, which makes them vulnerable to male violence, and above all in creating the economic conditions that continuously put women's lives at risk—for instance, immigration legislation that increasingly puts women's lives in danger. For, in addition to all the other dangers immigrants are facing, women are facing attacks on their bodies. This is not just about rape. People always want to concentrate on rape, and rape is horrible, but if we look at what is happening in Ciudad Juarez, for example, that isn't just rape. That is a massive attack on women.

FIONA: And war? You have written extensively about the devastation of militarism and "humanitarian intervention" for women, particularly in Africa. Relatedly, you have been very critical of the hypocrisy of the UN's claim to be standing up for women's rights while it approves military interventions. How do these connect to your conception of the changing relationship between women and the state under neoliberalism?

SILVIA: War is also an attack on women. We have a UN that claims to speak for women's rights while it also sanctions one war after another, knowing very well that in today's war, it is women and children who are the first to be killed. This is not news; at the time of the Vietnam War, already 80 per cent of those killed were civilians, and the most vulnerable to being killed were women and children. Institutions like the UN appear to advocate for women's rights as long as those rights are functional to the new forms of work that capital wants to inaugurate with women. And because of the crisis of the male command over women, the crisis of the male wage, the crisis of the male relationship with women, now the state—local and international—has to take over: there is a changing of the guard. In this changing of the guard, the state is taking over the role the man had, because he is now increasingly unemployed, because he is absent from the community because of migration, because the male position has been attacked with deindustrialization, and because in so many ways the social position that many men held has come under attack. Now the state has created a supplementary set of laws and initiatives, such as microcredit, to establish that direct control. Now there is less delegation and more direct command.

The Divisions among Us

FIONA: Like many people, I read *Caliban and the Witch* with a group of feminist activists immersed in different struggles. One of the things that really struck us was the point you make in the book about how the European witch hunt was a catalyst in a larger process of the accumulation of divisions—among women and men, children and adults, animals and humans, and so on. The painful divisions that often erupt between us often appear shocking and new, somehow, as though we are inventing new divisions as we go along. But the point that was politically important for us was the recognition that the apparent inability of movements to get beyond our divisions is not a magic product of troubled consciousness, but an unequivocally historical process.

SILVIA: Yes, that process begins but is not exhausted in the period of the witch hunts. When you look at the witch hunts, you find that new social legislation that inflamed divisions among people emerged in that period. It also appeared in the eighteenth and nineteenth centuries. At each point, you have a move towards the re-creation of a new type of femininity, a new type of masculinity, and the creation of new differences between women and men. Of course, division is a process that is adjusted depending on the context. It is one thing in Europe and another in Mexico, for example, because the work and forms of exploitation are different. If you look at changes in criminal laws, at the witch hunt campaigns, at changes in the official and high cultures, you find tremendous transformation in the way women and men are seen. What you find in these laws and the circulating imagery of women and men is really a proscriptive transformation about how women and men should behave, because they were accompanied by a series of designated punishments. Forms of social behaviour that had prevailed on a mass level were criminalized. I think that's what I try to show in the story I tell of the witch hunts: that there is a process of mass criminalization of very widespread, popular behaviour.

FIONA: What kinds of behaviour?

SILVIA: In relation to sexuality, for example. The control that women had over procreation. Or, for example, folk healing. This is the general context, but within it you also find a whole set of laws that deepened the division between women and men. And you begin to see two very separate spheres emerge. What *Caliban and the Witch* tries to point out is that the creation of divisions cements a certain kind of hierarchy, one that is first of all constructed by socio-economic and political means. It is constructed on the basis of a major transformation of the relationship that women and men have to capital. In other words, the fundamental terrain of all the differences in identity, behaviour, and practices—the root cause—is the change that begins to take place in how women and men relate to the means of subsistence, to capital, to the state. In that process, more and more women are being confined to the sphere of unpaid labour. They are not seen as workers, and so they are confined to forms of work that do not guarantee their capacity for subsistence. The kind of erosion that, even if they have jobs outside the home, even at the lowest echelon, there is no guarantee of survival.

This difference, which is built more and more over time, culminates in the nineteenth century with the rise of the nuclear family, where you have the man working for a wage and the woman doing unpaid labour. That is the material terrain on which the other differences, hierarchies, and power relationships are built. So, for example, it is the man who makes decisions about the sexuality of the woman. Obviously there is always a struggle. You never have a situation that is unilateral, where force only runs in one direction. But nevertheless, within the proletariat, the power is in a man's hands—power over a woman's body—as is the power to ruin a woman by saying, for example, that she is a slut, she is a prostitute, she's promiscuous.

In the book, I wrote about how these changes brought radical cultural transformations. The entire cultural view of women and men became steeped in an image of woman as pure passivity, with all the characteristics that come with it: docility, silence, obedience. This was a reversal of the image of women in the Middle Ages, when women were supposed to be more violent, more sexual, even sexually insatiable, and so on. The legacy of the witch hunts era brings a characterization of women that becomes functional to the fact that they have to become fundamentally subordinate to and dependent on men.

And, of course, there is a legal system that makes it increasingly difficult for women to have an independent legal existence. So this is more than ideology. You actually have a construction that is economic, legal, and cultural. You have the culture defining qualities, traits, and features that are functional to this image of women's subordination, to an ideal of dependence. Then you have legislation that makes it difficult for women to have an autonomous existence—to have citizenship in their own name, for example. You also have the material conditions of existence. In *Caliban*, I spoke of the fact that in some parts of sixteenth- and seventeenth-century Europe—in Germany, for example—women were forbidden from performing waged work. You can find records of women petitioning the local authorities, pleading, "Please, allow me to earn a living."

FIONA: What if they didn't have any means of support?

SILVIA: Well, perhaps they would go be a live-in maid or something, but they couldn't have the types of waged jobs men had, in the textile industry or whatever. So you find all kinds of women making petitions to the local authorities because they were widows. Also, women couldn't live alone. They had to attach themselves to some kind of family or to a husband. So there are actually very precise initiatives to construct divisions and hierarchy. This is not about difference, which could be implemented with equality. What we are talking about is ranking, subordination, degradation: she is a grade less.

The same goes for the relationship between humans and animals. The degradation of animals is very much part of the other side of the long process of enclosure, or, in other words, the beginning of the wage relation for men, and the beginning of dependency for women. But there is another side to enclosure, which is the separation of people from the natural world. And this separation has involved an incredible attack on people's lives, knowledge, power, and self-confidence. Daily contact with nature brings a tremendous sense of self-confidence. When you are in contact with nature, your powers grow. Nature is really the continuation of our bodies. And there is a whole kind of knowledge that you build through this contact with the sea, wind, and land. You feel part of a much broader world of forces that interact continuously with your life.

The moment you are taken away from that and you are thrown into a slum, or into a factory, there is an incredible mutilation and suffocation of your power. There is a tremendous process of pauperization of your body, of your self, of your imagination, of your knowledge. A whole world of knowledge disappears. A whole world of power and capacity disappears. And understanding this is something we need to integrate into the discourse on the capitalist enclosures. This degradation of our relationship with nature is not a separate issue: it is integral to the economic impact of enclosure. This loss becomes especially vivid when you look at all the stories in the Middle Ages in which animals are able to speak. In pre-capitalist times, animals were so often the protagonists of people's lives. Now they have been expunged. If you look at the literature of ancient Greece and pre-capitalist society, you find a lot of speaking animals. In *Caliban*, I mention the trials that were conducted against animals until the sixteenth century. There was fluidity between the animal and human worlds; it was a world where being a human did not prevent you from communicating with animals. And animals were attributed qualities that we now think of as uniquely human, and vice versa: human beings could appropriate and be thought to have powers that we only think of as animal powers.

With the enclosure movement, you have that separation. You are separated from nature, from animals. It is not only separation; a new system of ranking, hierarchies, and degradation is put in motion. So there is a whole degradation of the animal world, and this goes hand in hand with the degradation of women. And of course, you see during this shift how women came to be seen as animals. You also find at this time a degradation of the body. This is why I am very suspicious of the discourse of immaterial labour. I'm very suspicious of anything that puts the stress on immateriality. Who conceives of knowledge only in immaterial terms? Who conceives of the commons only in immaterial terms? The weight of history is too heavy. And there is a long history of persistent degradation of what is called the "material sphere," and this sphere always happened to refer to the world of animals, women, children, and the body in general.

The change in attitude towards children that comes with capitalist enclosure starkly shows this ranking. Children are now without reason: the little animals that can be beaten up, the ones whose labour power has to be created. They are just little animals in apprenticeship to become workers. Philippe Ariès, a famous sociologist who wrote a number of books on children, found that in the Middle Ages children were not seen as part of a different world than adults. The idea of children as something unique did not develop until much later. The representations of children at the time show them as little adults. The distance between adults and children was deepened by capitalism. Before, children were in all the spaces and times in which adults were. There was no sense of confining children to a special sphere. The idea of the little, innocent child who has to be protected is a product of capitalist culture. And with capitalism also comes the very punitive attitude towards the child, namely the idea that the child has to be broken. Protestant literature of the sixteenth and seventeenth centuries shows an obsession with the education of children, an obsession with forming a particular type of person. Once education came to be seen as a process of adaptation—to the law, the authorities, the future world of work—a whole new set of attitudes was introduced.

The Europeans exported these attitudes to the places they colonized. I encountered the work of a French missionary in seventeenth-century Canada who wrote about his contact with Indigenous tribes. He talks about how he taught them how to discipline their children. Until the moment comes when it is decided that the children will be beaten, the notion of beating up children is unknown. The same missionary educates these men to take power over women. Both ideas were deeply resisted.

All of this is part of a creation of ranks: of heads and of hands. It is part of a division where some command and are attributed a higher power, and some are commanded and seen as willing automatons. So every time we talk about de-materialization, my historical hair goes up. I don't find that language useful for going forward. I think we can say what we want to say about new forms of labour without rehashing ideas that risk carrying on the kind of degradation that has been so predominant historically.

FIONA: How do you think such world-changing ideas become absorbed to the extent that they appear to be eternal and natural, even though such rankings and degradations face constant challenges when you look closely?

SILVIA: I think they become absorbed because it's a process of continuous interaction between the economic and the cultural, the economic and the social. As people become increasingly dependent economically, they lose ground. And they have to renegotiate the relationship and the rules that go along with it.

FIONA: At the same time, paradoxically, these stories do show how long and unstable the process of absorption of these hierarchies, ideas, and practices actually was. It shows how much violence is behind what we see to be normal modes of behaviour and social organization, which is another theme in *Caliban* and throughout your work.

SILVIA: Yes, how long the resistance has been! People cannot live out of fixed cultural forms. Culture is always changing, and resistance has also changed; it's still there. In *Caliban* I document some parts of this resistance when I speak of the women in Peru who carried the struggle against the colonizers—who also brought persecution of women as witches—underground. They fled to the mountains and recreated autonomous communities of women there. In some cases these communities still exist today, despite the hell-bent means by which the colonizers tried to destroy them. The colonizers were never successful, and they still have to fight the communities today.

Confronting Fear

FIONA: Now that we are on the question of resistance, I'd like to ask about a story that you recount in *Caliban* about Basque fishing communities that successfully resisted the witch-hunting Inquisitors. In the story you recount, the Inquisitors appeared, ready to initiate a trial for witchcraft, and the community drove them out, for good. It is an amazing story, not least because it shows a spectacular instance of collective refusal of the witch hunters' campaign of fear. Sadly, the story also suggests that organized, collective resistance to the witch-hunting authorities was quite anomalous, as you point out in your book, throughout this long, violent period of persecution.

SILVIA: Yes, that is a fantastic story! I would point to two main reasons why this resistance was possible. The first was the tremendous solidarity among the men. These were people who lived all together for many months of the year, and together risked their lives in taking to the Atlantic to fish for cod. And we are talking about the sixteenth century here, when this work was extremely hard and perilous. So this example relates back to an earlier part of our discussion, when I was talking about communities of resistance under fascism. People in both cases knew each other's stories. There was an understanding that you depended on the person next to you and they depended on you. The Basque fishers lived this, as they sailed off into the

Atlantic Ocean to bring home the wealth on which they would live for the rest of the year. That also meant that for long periods of time, the women were alone in the community. It meant the women were very strong, very independent. It also meant that the men were extremely dependent on these women, because when they were gone the women took care of the community. They took care of the children, of the elderly, of the whole economy of the place. The women did everything, and for this they were a scandal. This is why, when the French Inquisitor Pierre Lancre went to the Basque Country, he declared, "This is a place of witches! This is a population where all the women are witches!" This was a place of witches because the women were very independent. They were not under the control of men, and they had developed, obviously, a very different kind of personality than the ideal of the submissive woman that the French Inquisitor had in mind. But it was this independence that the men relied on. They couldn't afford not to have the women in the community.

The other element was that this was a community very much organized around pre-capitalist concepts. In this community, your life was not organized around the daily discipline of waged labour. The men sacrificed greatly for several months, risking their lives daily, but then came home and lived off of the wealth. They came home, sold the fish, and lived off what they earned. They had a good time, with periods when they weren't working every day. So it was a community that sacrificed, but did not have the daily erosion of the spirit that comes with the daily discipline of waged work, and of having a boss over your head. They were very independent.

So from a capitalist bourgeois perspective, this was a highly undisciplined community. The women did not have the daily discipline of male authority, and the men did not have the daily discipline of the wage and the job. So you can imagine the kind of culture that was created in such a community. In the eyes of an Inquisitor, it was a culture that was obviously demonic, savage. The Inquisition's attempt to discipline this community through witch trials occurred three-quarters of a century after the colonization of Mexico. The Inquisitions in Mexico and Peru were the same as the ones in France and Spain. They read the same texts and communicated with each other. And from here you begin to have an exchange of assumptions, upon which the comparison of witches with the "New World" was built. The dominant image of this new world was filled with ideas about witches and witchcraft, images that connected witches to "savages" who were not disciplined by work according to the European mode. This image was transposed to read forms of behaviour at home. So the seventeenth century was a moment of profound change in Europe, as well as the colonies.

FIONA: And were there any other recorded cases where Inquisitors were expelled? Or cases where the communities, families, or friends of the accused women stood up to the Inquisitors on their behalf?

SILVIA: Yes, actually, there are other examples, but rather more limited. Most of the women who were accused lived alone or were married to men of the lowest status—wage labourers, which was almost like being a slave. These men had little power to protect women who were accused of being witches. But in some instances where the family of the accused woman had more power and where the men of the family acted, then she got away. In some instances, they whisked her away because they thought she would be accused. In other cases, they assaulted the prison where the women were being held—often a small village wouldn't have a real prison, just a small room fashioned into a prison. So there were a number of acts of resistance to the witch hunts, but these were individual cases. I think what is unique about the Basque case, at least from what I've read, is that it was a large group of men and it was organized. It wasn't just the husband, the brother, the sister, the father. So I think those characteristics made all the difference.

PART II

THEORIZING

3

DAVID HARVEY

Indignant Cities

RENOWNED urbanist and geographer David Harvey is Distinguished Professor of Anthropology at the City University of New York, and one of the most cited social theorists working today. He is a prolific writer, whose wide-ranging work has been pivotal to the theorization of global and urban change. Harvey's already substantial public profile widened considerably in the wake of the global financial meltdown of 2008, thanks to two books and numerous lectures that shed light on its causes and significance.

In our interview, Harvey discusses the role of fear in urban change, city politics, and the turn towards financialized capitalism. Our discussion begins with his reflections on how his move from England to Baltimore in the late 1960s influenced his thinking about city life, social change, and social justice. We continue with a discussion of the role of bourgeois fear of the masses in the shaping of urban redevelopment schemes, from Paris in the nineteenth century to New York City from the 1970s to today. While our conversation took place prior to the eruption of Occupy Wall Street in the fall of 2011, Harvey makes some highly relevant, and even prophetic, comments about the possible, and essential, emergence of a broad social movement of the indignant to articulate the needs and desires of both the dispossessed and the discontented.

Harvey has been writing about cities and social change for over four decades. He arrived in Baltimore at a moment of intense political upheaval in the US, and a year after the city was rocked by massive riots. In an effort to gain deeper insight into the crisis, Harvey embarked on a serious study of Marx's work to see how a philosophy devoted to understanding capitalism and social change would shed light on the remarkable changes taking place around the US and the world. Since then, his work has been preoccupied with bringing Marx's insights to the study of urban change and with urging Marxists to take seriously his contention that the city is a terrain of proliferating antagonisms and utopian possibilities. Harvey's sweeping critique of postmodern culture in the late 1980s catapulted him to world renown. But his work on cities and on capitalism's tendency towards recurrent crisis has been among his most illuminating and influential contributions to radical social thought and practice. Whether he is meeting with striking high school students in Santiago, Chile, or addressing an academic audience at the London School of Economics, Harvey's work reaches an increasingly wide audience inside and outside academic debates—an impressive achievement for a scholarly writer in an era of shaky but stubbornly dominant neoliberal common sense.

In our conversation, Harvey discusses how the modern city has historically been an arena of fear. But his reference point is not the familiar story of how the fears of ordinary city dwellers caused them to turn on one another. He urges us to think about bourgeois fear of the masses and how it created a whole way of thinking and feeling about the city and its dangers, shaping, for example, the wholesale redesign of Paris, the quintessential modern city. Harvey's analysis helps us to think about contemporary urban design, and how cities like New York can reveal the fears of the powerful.

Urban Unrest as an Impetus to Social Inquiry

FIONA: Could you talk about some of the key events and ideas that led you to focus much of your scholarly and political work on the modern city as site of revolutionary thought and action?

DAVID: The 1960s was a period in which something called the urban crisis was a big question. Of course, it wasn't really an urban crisis; it was a crisis of the inner cities. And it wasn't only a problem in the United States: it was also a problem in Britain. During the 1960s, there were strong urban social movements in places like France, and I think one of the underestimated aspects of the movement of '68, in Paris and elsewhere, was the neighbourhood movements, which were very strong. There was intense antagonism to the modernist project of reurbanization, which is rather beautifully captured in Jean-Luc Godard's movie *Two or Three Things I Know about Her*.

Clearly, the urban issue was a big issue, and I was moving from Britain to the United States. I arrived in the city of Baltimore a year after the urban uprisings that followed the assassination of Martin Luther King Jr. The National Guard had to bring in tanks to control the urban uprisings, and it seemed unreal to me to come into a new place like Baltimore where all this was going on and not pay attention to it. When I got to Johns Hopkins University, I found there were several projects in the universities that tried to get to the roots of the urban crisis, particularly on housing questions. I became involved in several research projects on housing, which brought me very close to looking at conditions in the inner city, such as the racism in housing markets and the predatory practices of the real estate sector in relationship to it. This really fascinated me. Reading about all the predatory practices around the foreclosures going on now, I see the same damn thing happening as was happening back then in the 1960s—although, of course, the mechanisms and techniques are slightly different. So I got involved, because it seemed like I was destined to do it. And I'm very glad I did.

Spaces of Hope and Fear

FIONA: One of your books is entitled *Spaces of Hope*, and it is also a book about the city. As you elaborate in many of your writings, the city has historically been a site of possibility for the assertion of freedom. Other urban scholars, such as Mike Davis, for example, have chronicled the ways in which the city is also a space of fear, showing how fear is used as a technology of political control. What do you think is the relationship between hope and fear in the city?

DAVID: Well, it's interesting. I suppose you could see it as a simple opposition. I tend not to see it that way. Real change is always pretty fearful. I think one of the problems in this country [the US] right now is that on one level people see the need for real change, but are too fearful to go for it. And that is not something that is imposed by the existing order. I think that is something much more internal. I think there's a sense in which all of us would rather live with the devil we know than tempt one that we don't know at all. I think there is a certain fear of change, so that when you talk about the politics of hope, you are talking about a politics of transformation, and, to cite the old Maoist adage, you can't make an omelette without breaking eggs. So it means that the dialectic of fear and hope is always very strong at transformative moments. I don't think you can see real change occur without a lot of fear. The big question is, how does that fear get articulated into action, as opposed to the kind of fear that generates paralysis? And I think that historically what you often see is a certain paralysis, which can suddenly be overcome, and then you get uprisings, which seem to come from nowhere! And I think political uprisings are the moments when the fear that is generating paralysis is suddenly turned into a fear that says, "We have got to change something and we're prepared to risk something, even though it is a fearful risk that we're undertaking."

FIONA: Can you give an example?

DAVID: I think one good example was that huge, worldwide anti-war demonstration that took place on February 15 of 2003, the size of which took everyone by surprise—including the people who participated! I think there was a sense of a real fear of an unnecessary war and of the ramifications of that war. And people suddenly felt that they had to change something to try and stop it. That particular demonstration didn't succeed, and the war ensued and continues to go on and on. I think, actually, the people who were fearful at that time had a right to be fearful, and it was fantastic that they turned out to take up that right. And in retrospect, it is one of the tragedies of this century that nobody listened, even if some of the protesters' objections were taken seriously. Everyone who turned out on that occasion did have an impact. The mainstream media, which up until that point had dismissed opposition to the invasion of Iraq as minimal, suddenly saw it. Even *The New York Times* acknowledged that this demonstration was an expression of global public opinion and that it had to be respected to some degree. It was interesting that after that date, the *Times*, which had really scoffed at anti-war demonstrators up until then, was one of the few publications to try to take at least some distance from the administration and its plan of going to war in Iraq.

The story makes me think of Henri Lefebvre's account, by the way, of the uprisings of 1968 in his book *The Eruption*. I think it is a very interesting one. He depicts these uprisings as a moment when suddenly everybody overcame the fear that produces passivity and was prepared to engage with the fear that goes with action. And the reason he calls it "The Eruption" is that it was a moment—and he thinks all revolutions are momentary events of this kind—when people saw possibility that they did not see in their ordinary lives. I think it has always been very interesting to listen to the commentaries of those who were deeply involved in the '68 movement and hear many people say things like, "I really don't know quite what I did and why I did it." And I think they have a hard time rationalizing it subsequently.

FIONA: Why is that, do you think? Because of its collective nature?

DAVID: Partly because of its collective nature, and partly because the moment of political possibility breaks down, and now you are reabsorbed into the dominant practices of everyday life. You can't see why you would have gone out there and done some of the things you did.

FIONA: Your writing on the political turbulence of nineteenth-century France raises many interesting ideas about, among many other things, the various ways in which bourgeois fear of the urban proletariat became inscribed onto the organization of the city of Paris. Your reflections on ruling-class fear raise a surprising set of questions, because fear is usually attributed to the lives and political subjectivities of the popular classes. So my question is: How does the modern revolutionary period in Second Empire France narrate a story of ruling-class fear?

DAVID: It is, quite simply put, fear of the Other. What was stunning to me about Second Empire Paris was that the Other was not a racially distinct group, but was seen as a biologically inferior class of the French. So we now think of racism as something that is clearly directed at people of colour. But actually, that interpretation was a racist interpretation of what the aristocracy and the bourgeoisie gave to the working classes. And I think this goes back to the idea that the ruling class always wants to think that it is a ruling class by nature—that they have a natural right to rule. So any challenge to their rule by anybody else is treated as an uprising of the unnatural. So I think this racist view of the working class at that time was at the centre of a lot of bourgeois fear, but was also a way for the bourgeoisie to homogenize its interest, to collectivize its fears.

Stories of Fear

FIONA: To socialize their fears, in a sense? To turn their own fears about threats to their power outward and render them shared fears?

DAVID: Yes. It becomes a class phenomenon, a way in which the ruling classes would take their collective stance in industry, or whatever, and say "This is our collective" in order to collectivize what are obviously rather fragmented interests. I always like the passage in Marx's *Capital* where he talks about how, during the revolutionary tumult of 1848, all segments of the bourgeoisie dropped their hostilities, got together, and said, "We have to sock it to the working class and prevent them absolutely from expressing any power." One thing they would do is spread stories about conspiracies. The Parisian bourgeoisie had a great fear of the sewers, where they imagined lurked all these ghastly human beings, who they thought were going to arise and create revolution on the streets of Paris. It follows, then, that when Georges-Eugène Haussmann [the principal figure in the redesign of Paris] built new sewers, he had to allay bourgeois fears by giving tours of the sewers. There are great pictures of boats sailing through the sewers, just to reassure the bourgeoisie that there were no monsters lurking there.

FIONA: So they believed their own story?

DAVID: Oh, yes! They were terrified of what lay underground in Paris. This is where, in many ways, the phrase "the underground" comes from. And during the Paris Commune [of 1871], the communards were described as those that had come out of the sewers, like they were ragged dogs that needed to be shot down and killed.

FIONA: It is interesting how the vermin language pops up over and over in historic moments of fear. And, even more relevant to our discussion, how this language suggests a very urban kind of fear.

DAVID: Yes. People talk about underground conspiracies. Why do conspiracies have to be underground? Well, it comes out of that historical fear.

Fears of the Seen and the Unseen

FIONA: Interesting. What about the other parts of the built environment or urban infrastructure? Do you think the shape of the cities was changed as a result? Can you read those fears on the shape of the city that emerged out of that period?

DAVID: Well, the fears are of course located in the notion of the slum or the territories of the impoverished—the *bidonvilles* in France—and of course, now you'd say the same thing about the Brazilian *favelas*. There's a fear of those spaces, which seem to be lacking in social control. So, for example, in Second Empire Paris, when Haussmann cleared out a lot of those allegedly threatening spaces, it was partly done by bringing light and air into the city. On the one hand, there was a lot of concern about health, controlling cholera and disease. But at the same time, it was a strategy of social control. You clear out the spaces that are hard to survey, where it's hard to keep social control. And you get people into housing that is transparent.

FIONA: This is a bit of a geographical and historical leap in the conversation, but one place you can see this logic of transparency you speak of starkly at work today is in Israeli military interventions in Gaza. Spokespeople for the Israel Defense Forces talk about Gaza as an opaque, unknown territory, full of warrens and hiding places and so on. Exposing what cannot otherwise be seen is a strategy of attempting to create a tightly controlled urban experience. Which is, of course, a fragile aspiration, no matter how asymmetrical the relationship is between the visible and the unseen.

DAVID: You could probably map spaces of fear in the city, if you wanted to see it that way, by going to the middle classes. In the 1960s, for example, I was astonished to find that many people who lived in Baltimore County would never, ever go into the city. Never, ever. If they absolutely had to go there, they would speed down the causeway to get where they had to go, directly to the courthouse or whatever. But they were terrified of the central city.

FIONA: Did people ever express what they were so afraid of, exactly? Did they imagine they would be jumped, or was it an ambient, generalized fear of the unknown?

DAVID: Yes, both.

FIONA: In your elaboration of a geographical theory of social change, you have written widely on both post-war suburbanization and the effect of McCarthyism on US political culture. Would you say that this notion of bourgeois fear is helpful for understanding these two seemingly unrelated processes of McCarthyism and suburbanization?

DAVID: I don't think it's simply a matter of bourgeois fear at this point. When you say "fear," there is something rather irrational about it. I think there is a bourgeois strategy—a capitalist class strategy, if you will—of keeping social, economic, and political control. I see McCarthyism, and to some degree the kind of repressions on freedom of speech that happened after 9/11 in the US, as part of a strategy—a conscious strategy, to try to mobilize fear for a political purpose.

And that fear was a fear of the left. It was a fear of socialism, of communism, of government, of interventionism in the economy and social life in general. So this fear gets mobilized as part of a political strategy, which, of course, incorporates the paranoia of some groups in the population. We can see this happening right now in the health care debates, in the paranoia that some groups have about government involvement in health care delivery. So you get these ridiculous statements like "I don't want the government to intervene in my Medicare!" The fear of state involvement can be mobilized. But this is mobilized for political reasons.

Suburban Fears

DAVID: In regards to suburbanization, by the same token, the idea that after World War II there was a drive to get back to a full-employment economy produced a big problem: how are you going to do it? What are people going to be fully employed on? The automobile industry was one possibility. But then if you have automobiles, you have to have highways upon which they can run, and an urban system that encourages automobile use and eventually mandates the car as the necessary attribute of every household that wants to participate in the basics of American life. For many, the car was necessary to access schools, shopping centres, work opportunities, and so on. So suburbanization dealt with the whole full-employment problem and became one of the ways in which the tremendous productive capacity the United States developed during World War II could be employed on a new, peaceful project. But this meant that people had to become homeowners, so they had to give people access to homeownership. Which, of course, made people very concerned about their asset values, the value of their property. Homeownership became a main form of savings for ordinary people. And of course, people became very enamoured with private property, so it extended, if you like, the political basis of support for the capitalist system, which is based on private property and individual property rights.

So there was a fear, if you want to call it that, or recognition in World War II that you couldn't go back to the conditions of the 1930s. I don't know how many millions of people were in the armed services. But you had a lot of people coming back who knew how to use guns. They had fought for liberty, and all the rest of it. They had seen many of their compatriots die in that process. If you brought them back and said, "Oh, well, you fought for all of that and now you're going to be unemployed," you would have had a revolutionary situation on your hands. I think everybody with political power among the capitalist class knew that, and was desperately concerned with preventing it from happening. Full employment became necessary, and cutting the working class in on part of the wealth of the country became part of the deal. What was known as the Compact of Detroit—a well-paid working class that could have a suburban standard of life, drive some of the cars they were making, and so on—was going to be the basis of political stability.

FIONA: And the end of decently paid jobs for women that had opened up during the war, and the beginning, for not just a few, of lonely exile in the suburban home.

DAVID: Yes. Return to the home, as feminists of the seventies called it, the "place with no name." This suburban lifestyle was one of the central critiques women had in the 1960s.

FIONA: It is interesting when you put it like that. The conditions of life in the suburbs became an impetus for a revolutionary movement.

DAVID: That was also where white youths became discontented, and in a sense, it became an impetus of the student movement of the sixties, which demanded a different kind of urbanism. The youth looked to the city, and found themselves allying with minorities in the city. After that you get the '68 movement in the United States.

Crisis Cycles

FIONA: Your analysis of the rise of neoliberalism situates New York City's fiscal crisis in the 1970s as a seminal turning point. You show how the crisis was harnessed to radically restructure the urban and national economies, and how the transformation of the city provided a stage for the global project of neoliberalism. This crisis erupted amid a period of intense social upheaval, whereby emancipatory movements of various kinds—feminism, labour, black power, urban justice, and so on—posed a serious challenge to the entrenched organization of class relations, both in the US and internationally. To what extent was the response of the dominant class to New York City's fiscal crisis also a response to that challenge?

DAVID: There's no question that the response to the fiscal difficulties of New York City in 1975 was partly the response of a white power structure that was fearful, to go back to the fear question, of rising black power. So I think there's no question that it had a very strong racial component. At the same time, it was also about disciplining labour and disciplining the population of New York City as a whole. In a way, it was a pioneer structural adjustment program. When I say this, though, I also think it was a pioneer experiment. I don't think the capitalist class knew exactly what to do. I don't think they sat down and said, "Hey, let's do this!" I think it was more like, "My God, there's this mess. Let's try this, let's do that." But by the time they came to the end of the 1970s and they looked at what they had done to New York, they said, "Hey, this is a pretty good idea." And when Mexico got into unmanageable debt in 1982, they said, "Well, hey, let's go do to Mexico what we did to New York City."

I'm not sure how much the other issues of the time entered in. There was, after all, quite a strong environmental movement emerging around then. The feminist movement, of course, and the student movement still had a lot of heft to them. When did the Kent State repression happen? It was in 1970. We talk about the sixties, but the seventies were a very contentious decade, too.

FIONA: Because a lot of struggles and ideas were being put into motion by the seventies, past the emergent or insurgent phase of the previous decade?

DAVID: Yes, and that is when the capitalist class started to react. That's when all this anti-corporate legislation started to go through: environmental protection, consumer protection, and health and safety legislation, for example. And it was Nixon who signed it into law! He said, "We're all Keynesians now." And it was at this time that the capitalist class really started to reorganize itself. When the New York fiscal crisis came about, some of the leading figures behind that crisis were investment bankers like the Rockefellers, City Bank, and so on. They were the ones who were experimenting with that situation.

FIONA: I've seen a number of accounts of this period that emphasize the symbolic importance of imposing austerity on New York City, because it is a progressive city with a strong, radical tradition that could be dampened by some neoliberal discipline. Do you think this was the case? Do you think that New York City was of great symbolic importance to the neoliberal project of privatization and deregulation at this time?

DAVID: I don't think it was seen deliberately that way. I don't know if the power of the municipal unions was greater in New York than it was in San Francisco, Baltimore, or Detroit. Maybe it was. But nationwide, a lot of cities were going through similar difficulties. There was an urban fiscal crisis across the US in the mid-1970s. In Baltimore we went through it. There were teachers' strikes, hospital workers' strikes, garbage workers' strikes, tremendous difficulties in the city. The significance of New York was simply that the depth of the fiscal crisis was greater there than it was anywhere else, for a variety of reasons, one of which had to do with the fact that investment bankers in the 1960s had taught the New York City government how to play games with their budget in such a way as to make a lot of money fungible. Investment bankers had encouraged New York to go into debt because they had seen it as a great source of income in the 1960s and 1970s. In a sense, the bankers played a very important role in creating the fiscal crisis. And to the degree that there is a special relationship between the New York administration and Wall Street figures, I think at this time it got deeper and became more of a problem.

FIONA: My next question is a two-part question about the current crisis in global capitalism. What do you think has been the role of fear in this present crisis? And what does this role tell us about the possibilities for revolutionary transformation?

DAVID: I'm not so sure how to think about the role of fear in this case. I would say that the big problem over the past twenty years, at least, has been that—and the World Bank and International Monetary Fund often say this—the world is awash in surplus liquidity, and nobody knows where to put it for profitable investment. So you may say, "Okay, well, there is a fear that it won't work." But what this led into was the search for speculative outlets for capital, which fed upon themselves. So people started to speculate in asset values, and that speculation started to become self-propelling. I think it was more living in a fantasy world, and the tremendous hubris that came with command over some of the new financial instruments: derivatives, and collateralized debt obligations, and all the rest of it. Now, I think that many people either lived in a politics of denial, which is not uncommon, or they knew it was going to all come apart but figured they could get out before it did. And this is the famous philosophy of *après moi le déluge*—I take as much as I can. And a lot of those people who did make megabucks did get out. Today they're sitting in the Bahamas, sailing their yachts now and again. They did fine out of the whole thing. It was a bunch of predatory practices.

FIONA: And what about the dominant way in which the crisis was talked about during the first year? Fear of decline, global systemic collapse, unemployment, the jobless recovery, and so forth. On many different registers, fear became a central term in the media. Everybody had something to be deathly frightened of.

DAVID: Yes, after the crash, obviously, people are burned and are very fearful. As the crash carried over into unemployment and insecurity and all those other issues, like people losing their pensions, there was a lot of fear. It was a situation where FDR's commentary "There's nothing to fear but fear itself" certainly resonated. Now everyone is trying to talk people out of being fearful, urging investors, "Put your money back into the market. Everything is going to be okay!" Now we get all this chatter about economic "green shoots" everywhere, trying to assure people, even as unemployment is rising.

Now, how much unemployed people's fears will actually produce a political movement is a really interesting question. I think it's the case that there will be a situation parallel with that of the Great Depression of the 1930s: you have the stock market crash of 1929, and it was not until 1932 or '33 that the social movements had become so huge that Roosevelt had to do something really dramatic. And I think that is what it's going to take. If we have unemployment that continues to rise—and there's talk from [former Federal Reserve Chairman Alan] Greenspan that it will go above 10 per cent and go way, way into next year—and mass unemployment is perpetuated, I suspect that people will start to convert the sort of fear that leads to passivity into a fear that leads more into an activist orientation. But at that point, I think that the capitalist class interest will consolidate into how to prevent anything of significance from happening. It will probably try to do it through all sorts of tactics, including fear mongering and talking about socialism and communism or whatever. And we could well be in for some rather ugly repression, which will try to forestall any kind of radical transformation. What is so interesting to me is that the exit for this crisis, at this time, is about trying to restore the status quo.

FIONA: For whom?

DAVID: For the capitalist class.

FIONA: Restore it to what it was?

DAVID: Restore the situation. Put the banking system back to where it was before. Give the banks the power to leverage, which they're doing. Don't regulate too much, and if you do, then do it in such a way that it is Teflon regulation.

Alliances of the Dispossessed and the Discontented

FIONA: Given this grim scenario, do you see any possibility of change in the opposite direction? Obviously it is impossible to predict anything precise, but where, if anywhere, do you see it? Given how many people are losing jobs and homes while they drown in debt, do you see any new combinations of the dispossessed emerging out of this crisis?

DAVID: I'm not able to predict where it's going to come from. Who would have predicted the social movements that erupted in Bolivia? It is hard to predict. One of the things I will say, however, is that for real change to occur, it's going to require a fairly wide alliance. And it will require people who are really prepared to shed their conventional wisdoms and embrace more radical politics. One of the things that is very different now from, say, the 1930s is that in the thirties, there certainly were many people in what you might call the intelligentsia who saw many different kinds of possibilities. That is really not the case as I see it today. I think that the intelligentsia in the US, for example, is so locked into its conventional politics that most of them are neoliberal without knowing it, or fringe neoliberal. A real revolutionary transformation is going to require people with technical expertise and scientific expertise to join the revolutionary movement. Some may be willing to do so—particularly if it addresses environmental issues, because I think on those sorts of issues you'll probably get a lot of scientists with you. And you need to get a lot of people who are inside the bureaucracy who are prepared. You need dissident elements in the intelligentsia, inside the bureaucracy, in science and technology and technological development. You need dissident elements prepared to support a social movement that may come from the dispossessed.

FIONA: An expression that I heard recently was "contestational biologists"— biologists who are interested in the collective reorganization of science and technology.

DAVID: Yes, there are people like that around. There is this segregation that exists between different groups and different situations. My good friend Peter Marcuse is fond of talking about an alliance between the discontented and the dispossessed. I think that the discontented are just as important as the dispossessed. But for the dispossessed, there is much greater urgency for political action. I personally can't claim I'm dispossessed. I have a comfortable life, in some ways. So why would I go out and join a revolutionary movement? Because I think we are headed towards disaster. I think we are headed towards a rather ugly world, even uglier than it has been. And I don't see how anybody who has any kind of conception of what humanity could be about could continue to say that this system is the most adequate system for delivering even elementary things, like health care, to the mass of the people. Our present system can't do it, and it won't do it without a revolutionary transformation. So I see a revolutionary transformation as absolutely essential. I'm part of the discontented. And I think an alliance between the discontented and the dispossessed is very important to construct.

FIONA: The Zapatistas talk about anguish. Anguish is a kind of bridge.

DAVID: Yes. I think that Michael Hardt and Antonio Negri usefully draw on a Spinozist notion of indignation, which I think is a very good term, powerful. How many people around are indignant enough with the way things are and say that things have absolutely got to change? It has got to be sooner rather than later.

FIONA: So the right to indignation is important. The Right to the City, the Right to Indignation.

DAVID: Yes. I remember sitting with quite a conservative figure in Britain a while ago who had been a supporter of Thatcher. He was telling me that he had to get used to the fact that a homeless person was sleeping under the steps at his house. At some point, he started bringing him coffee in the morning, and other things. And as he recounted this story, at one point he said, "I supported Margaret Thatcher and I believed in a lot of the things she stood for, but frankly, I don't want to live in a world where I have to come out every morning and see this homeless person. And I don't want the police to take him away. I want a world in which this guy can have a decent life." I think there are a lot of people out there who have political loyalties to the left and to the right who would say, "I will join the party of indignation if you will."

4

NANDITA SHARMA

Terror and Mercy at the Border

NANDITA SHARMA is an activist-scholar whose work focuses on shifting border regimes under neoliberal globalization. She has been active in No Borders movements for many years, and she also teaches sociology at the University of Hawai'i. Sharma's writing and research have focused on the politics of global labour migration and the state regulation of people's lives through national border regimes. In our interview, she shares her thoughts on the significance of contemporary migration politics and practices in our paradoxical era of increasingly open markets and closed borders. In this era, migrants, and especially people moving across borders without state authorization, have been constructed as objects of fear and loathing. Our conversation focuses on the significance of the planetary movement of people under conditions of escalating austerity and dispossession, ongoing war, and border security obsessions. Such conditions have provided political entrepreneurs with a ripe environment to exploit people's fears of increasing scarcity and competition, leading to eruptions of anti-migrant xenophobia and nationalist panic attacks. In this context, border crossers have come to represent objects of loathing and fear, and the border itself is portrayed as a site of security that has spun out of control.

Much of our conversation reflects on how this emphasis on the border as a site of control, fear, and coercion has resonated in popular discourses around human mobility. Sharma shares her forthright critiques of the emergence of strange coalitions among feminists, states, and right-wing activists dedicated to fighting human trafficking, pointing to the conservative, coercive, and anti-migrant implications of this seemingly emancipatory politics. Whether it is intended or not, the dominant idea that propels contemporary anti-trafficking politics, Sharma argues, is the notion that because there is exploitation in the movement of people, migration must be halted. This is a dangerous claim, she contends, that only serves to make migrants—especially those made most vulnerable to exploitation by the documentation requirements themselves—even more exposed to the coercive power of states and employers. While crisis may be an impetus for migration, Sharma argues, it is necessary to understand that migration is also a way in which people deal with crisis.

Sharma traces her radical critique of our bordered world to an upbringing in which she was immersed in anti-colonial thought and activism. She recalls how the anti-colonial movement's rejection of imperialist logics encouraged her to think about, and then beyond, the national imaginaries that borders demarcate. This inspired Sharma to turn her attention to developing a perspective on struggles around migration that starts not from the point of view of the border enforcer—the nation—but from the point of view of the border crosser. Her work with undocumented and indentured migrants trying to survive in an increasingly fortified North America encouraged Sharma to view the border as a technology of power, from the perspective of the needs of people on the move. From this viewpoint, Sharma argues, we can begin to recognize the border zone as both a concrete and a symbolic space of control, and a demarcation of belonging whose purpose is to secure its own security. And this, she contends, is how the material and symbolic role of border controls and bordered thinking facilitates the increasingly differentiated application of terror and mercy. Grappling with this dialectic of terror and mercy is a central aspect of Sharma's thinking on the key questions of mobility, nationality, and globality. Throughout our conversation, she explains the different ways in which this dialectic plays out on the real and metaphorical borderlands of national belonging.

FIONA: Tell me a bit about your background. What experiences, events, and political histories have nourished your thinking and led you to devote so much of your scholarly and political work to thinking critically about the politics of borders, nationalism, and the dynamics of human mobility?

NANDITA: I'm trying to remember when I realized nationalism was a problem instead of a solution. I was raised within a Third World nationalist milieu, where having your independent nation-state was seen as necessary for liberation. Concepts like self-determination and autonomy were all-important concepts, and they were ideas I didn't question at that time as having a referent. I don't remember asking, "Who is self-determinant and autonomous? Who gets to make those decisions?" Instead, I was caught in a wholesale acceptance of liberal notions of democracy, where the state is understood as the vehicle of democracy. I was raised in a very odd setup. My father was a Marxist of the Maoist variety. My mother was a very devout Hindu whose parents were very active in the Congress Party approach to Indian independence from Britain. This political mix combined with my parents' and grandparents' stories about British colonization. This is what I heard throughout my entire childhood. I heard about how important the Indian nation-state project was to them, and my mother and father would both tell me that they supported other liberation struggles, like those of blacks in South Africa and Indigenous people in Canada. But then I realized that there was something not quite so democratic about this process when I encountered a book by Marxist scholars and activists called *The Difficult Dialogue: Marxism and Nationalism*. Going to university and getting access to texts like that one has been invaluable for me. I'm always very leery about anti-academic discourses. The university did radicalize me.

I came to understand nationalism as a problem when I was working with people without status in Canada. I didn't accept the liberal argument that the state had the right to determine people's status, and I became very interested in working with people classified as temporary residents because of how this designation worked as part of a capitalist system. The Third World liberationist answer to this problem has always been: these people don't really want to be here, so we should work for independence. But when you actually talk to migrant workers, many will tell you that their biggest concern is not building the nation "back home." I found that much of their working life was actually in Canada, and this provoked some new questions. If most of a migrant's life is spent in Canada, the US, or wherever, and they've come to see themselves as part of this society, what are the mechanisms that deny them that? How does it come to be that they are always seen as a problem, as a threat to that society? So I started to critique this notion of "society" that is used by both social movements and academia as an unquestioned unit. Working with people who are always classified as a threat to society made me question what society is if there are people living here who are classified as a threat: sex workers, drug users, the unemployed, single mothers, and so on. If you counted all those people out, you would wonder, who is society, then?

I came to see a big convergence of the left and the right on migration, both of which perceive it as always bad, always disruptive. It's bad for children, for women, for the family—just really moralistic ways of interpreting migration. But many of the migrants I spoke to feel very accomplished, that they have done this huge thing in their life, which they never thought possible. They have encountered all kinds of difficulties, and yet they are supporting others. So I do not want to romanticize displacement and migration, but rather to talk about these people as creating new societies and worlds. What is this desire to always tether them to the nation, whether it is the one back home, from a Third World liberation perspective, or as the ever-present threat, from the dominant First World view? I realized that none of those stories dealt with the migrants themselves. They were completely left out of the story. More recently, I've become fascinated with the idea of "new worlds"—precisely because it is so wrapped up with colonialism—and the idea that new worlds were created by colonization. Those new worlds were created out of violence, and out of displacement, but they are not only that. They have a more complex legacy. They are also new worlds that people recognize themselves in. They don't see these places as "not home."

An Initiation in Violence

FIONA: Is the analytic problem you identify here that movement "from below" is itself understood as a signal of oppression and exploitation, rather than the conditions under which movement takes place: unevenly, violently, and by way of dispossession?

NANDITA: Maybe a big part of how nationalism works is through this idea that we are going to create a perfect space that everyone wants to live in. All nationalisms require a fantasy of a "perfect homeland," to borrow a term from Ghassan Hage, because the homeland is not perfect, and therefore someone always has to be positioned as the problem. Once this problem has been dealt with, the story goes, everything will be fine. So maybe this idea of the perfect space that nobody is ever going to want to leave is actually an outcome of nationalist thinking, instead of just a desire for home. Maybe there has never been a human society where people want to leave. Leaving may be the result of some kind of crisis and a resolution to that crisis, rather than its cause. The idea of creating a perfect society that no one will ever want to leave is rooted in patriarchal desires for omnipotence.

FIONA: A nationalist narrative that advertises itself in the image of home, family, security, and safety?

NANDITA: And conceptions of nationalism are reliant on notions of a natural home, which guide our emotional, material, and physical ties, and one couldn't possibly have those same feelings for anywhere else. I think those are the narratives that drive the notion that migration is bad and must be stopped in our perfect world.

No Borders activists are commonly told they are delusional utopians. But a No Borders perspective understands migration to be induced by crisis, but also as a resolution to crisis. I see it as an anti-utopic project, because it is not a projection, but something people are making happen already. I don't want to underestimate the power of borders, and much of my work is meant to show that the nation-state has definitely not weakened under processes of capitalist globalization—that the nation-state is perhaps the first and one of the main regulatory mechanisms for capitalism, and the regulation of borders is a growing feature of our lives. I would say that the No Borders movement is not about utopia, but about democratizing a process that is already taking place, making it safer, and taking away one of the key mechanisms of labour control, which is citizenship status. In that sense, the No Borders movement is trying to undermine capitalist institutions, but it is also naming a practice that people are enacting every day already.

We have open borders in the sense that people are crossing them. We don't have open borders in the sense that when the poor cross the border, it hits them in the face. Both the rich and the poor are crossing borders on an unprecedented scale. Border controls are much more operative once people have crossed the physical borderline. This is the major, if often invisible, mechanism of border controls. The No Borders movements are trying to deal with proliferating internal borders. Poor people are made vulnerable through that act of crossing. It is that vulnerability that we would like to eliminate.

FIONA: The prevailing image of borders is of physical barriers at a demarcated line: walls, checkpoints, and the violence that goes into producing the line itself. How does the material border extend into, and help produce, a more general collective consciousness of national space and what it stands for?

NANDITA: I think the vulnerability that is introduced at that actual border is a kind of initiation. I don't at all want to underestimate the enormous violence that is done at that national border in terms of the deaths that occur and the brutality that is visited upon the bodies and minds of people who are trying to cross. But at the same time, we have an unprecedented human migration, an unprecedented number of people crossing national borders, so I think that the major accomplishment of the border restrictions that have intensified over the last couple of decades has not necessarily been to lessen people's mobility per se, but to render them vulnerable, weak, and subject to violence: the violence of employers, the nation, and nationalists. So what I've argued in my work is that border controls are largely ideological, because they are not meant for, and certainly do not accomplish, the restriction of people's mobility in the broader picture.

What they do accomplish is restricting their access to the protections, rights, and entitlements that are, formally at least, given to citizens and permanent residents in a country like Canada. But also, it is a way to continue the belief that this space exists for those who can claim some sense of national membership. And this means that always keeping some people in a position where they're not going to be part of society, and where they are going to be labelled threats to society, serves multiple purposes. Obviously, it cheapens their labour. It weakens their ability to fight against abuses. But it has also strengthened the sense of entitlement of nationalists. This is the dialectic always at play at the border.

FIONA: So do you think in that sense that the way we think the border works is fetishized?

NANDITA: I think it works as a kind of patriarchal omnipotence. It says, "I can control the border, and your existence across the line is evidence that I've lost control." This is clear in anti-migration rhetoric, which insists that the border is out of control. This is the nationalist patriarch flipping out because the object of his control has defied him. This dialectic of order and defiance is occurring at the border and inside nation-states when you have a group of migrants who have defied the will of the nation to control space. Migrants, while being rendered completely vulnerable members of society, are created as a problem because of their wilfulness and their defiance. This is a paradox always at play in the story of border crossing. The reversal also happens, wherein you have a group of nationalists who feel totally empowered by their national status, and feel comforted knowing they are connected with a state that is going to back them. At the same time, they are frothing with rage, because they feel this privileged status has been defied, and that they must respond with violence to regain control.

And then you get a parallel argument on the left, which says that migrants are weak and victims only, and we can rescue them by granting them membership in the nation. In this way, both positions are, paradoxically, operating in parallel universes, orbiting within the same logic. If you think the migrant is defiant and wilful, then you punish her. If you think the migrant is weak and a victim, then you allow him entry into your rightful existence.

FIONA: How does this dynamic relate to the dialectic of terror and mercy that plays a central role in your conceptualization of contemporary global migration politics?

NANDITA: The most non-radical response to people's need to move is the typical liberal claim, "Well, the good ones need to be able to get in." This depends on how you define the "good ones," whether that means they are total victims of political persecution, like the refugee or the female victim of trafficking, or the hard-working, tax-paying migrants. These are sly ways in which nationalist consciousness maintains control over people's movement. The "bad migrant" is always excluded. But the political right has an even more limited version of the good migrant. They say, "We should get the one with the MBA instead of the factory worker." Instead of asking who gives us the right to control people's movement, liberals typically respond by saying, "We'll just expand the definition of the good migrant." But who said it was our space in the first place?

Alternative Routes

FIONA: Designating the nation in this way, as a "safe space in a hostile world," involves extending hostility to those designated as "outside." Over the last decade, much has been written about the figure of the migrant as the new revolutionary subject of twenty-first-century global modernity. It is a designation that resonates in our era of increasingly strident border controls, mass displacement, and the grinding anxiety wrought by social precarity. So what does the figure of the migrant tell us about our current historical moment?

NANDITA: I find talking about migrants as "figures" of escape, transgression, and even resistance to be extremely problematic, because it objectifies migrants and imposes a meaning on their actions that is not necessarily self-defined. Having said that, I would also say that the act of migrating (and the people migrating for multiple reasons) does challenge the current world order. Especially when people migrate without official permission. This is something born of necessity, but the fact that it happens and that it happens increasingly in a world where most legal avenues of migration are being shut down is politically significant. The act of crossing a national border without official permission can be read as an act of challenging the world order, even if that is not the intent of the person crossing. It may not be resistance. Many people may well wish to join that world order. But it is a challenge to the prevailing order.

The raison d'être of the state is to produce order, and we call states failed states when they cannot produce order anymore. So it comes as no surprise that power would need to absolutely vilify and criminalize "the migrant," and turn her or him into a fearful figure. In a period when people are challenging the ability of the state to maintain order, the punishment of the migrant is one of the ways in which the state demonstrates its ability to assert order. I've written a lot about how the punishing of migrants is designed to demonstrate state power rather than stop migration. The claim to be imposing "order at the border" is thoroughly ideological. I don't think the "order at the border" discourse is ultimately aimed at ending undocumented immigration.

This is a major reason why the trafficking discourse is so problematic. Whether it is the state, Christian fundamentalists, or radical or liberal feminists doing the talking, the whole discussion around trafficking has turned the most sympathetic migrants into a problem. And it has done it in the trickiest and most awful way. The only people migrants can turn to, the ones with the capacity to deliver them across borders, are facing the greatest penalties for helping people move. I don't see feminists who support anti-trafficking working to find alternative routes for women and children to use so that they can bypass the existing for-profit trafficking system. If people's concern really is about the vulnerability of women and children who want to migrate, you would think that the logical thing would be to organize a movement that would get them across borders. This is happening, but those advocating anti-trafficking are not the ones carrying it out.

FIONA: How do such damaging inconsistencies function?

NANDITA: The driving idea is that it is migration that makes women and children vulnerable, and that the home space, ideologically defined as the space of the nation, is safe. It is supposed to protect you. Yet there is no discussion within the anti-trafficking discourse that for people coming from Poland, Nigeria, Thailand, and so on, those states are not protecting the vast majority of the population from anything. They are actually making people extremely vulnerable. There are many ideologies in the world today that are designed to have us believe that migration is, in and of itself, a problem. In turn, this reinforces the goodness of the state at the very time that nation-states in the First World are preventing people from moving safely. It fortifies the same institutions that are actually the problem for migrants. I believe we really do live in a global society today, and one of the ways in which hierarchies are maintained is through migration controls. Controlling people's freedom of movement is part and parcel of the neoliberal world order. So either preventing people from moving, or making them enormously vulnerable once they move, is one way that these hierarchies are managed.

FIONA: I see that the US Department of Defense has designated fighting human trafficking as a key mission. The scary-sounding terminology of "trafficking" gives the impression of a benevolent state dedicated to fighting social injustice and exploitation of the vulnerable.

NANDITA: And benevolent activists complement a benevolent state. Both are saying that migration is bad for you. For instance, the US government sponsors ad campaigns abroad that aim to discourage migration, because it is dangerous. So "don't migrate" travels from the far right to the left. Even within the left, you have people saying, "Maybe migration is just not good for people." In this way, migrants are turned into complete victims. It is a message to maintain existing hierarchies, all with the caveat that the message isn't going to prevent anyone from moving and everyone knows it. It is only going to make the people who move enormously vulnerable.

FIONA: Why is trafficking such a compelling narrative of mobility and exploitation? Why is it of particular concern to the Christian right?

NANDITA: For the Christian right, it is trafficking's absolute conflation with sex work, even though the vast majority of migrants are never involved in the sex industry. This is never mentioned. It is again about using migrants to advance another agenda, which is its appeal for a segment of the radical feminist movement that has focused on trafficking as well. These movements use migrants as a justification for their existence: they claim to be saving women and children.

And what happens to those who are identified as victims of sex trafficking? The vast majority of them are deported. So the anti-trafficking discourse also turns deportation into an act of benevolence. Because, of course, when you say someone has been trafficked, the image conjured up is of someone who has been kidnapped, chained to a boat, plane, or truck, and forced into slavery. The logical thought is that of course that person would want to go home. The people themselves are thereby completely removed from the process that they have just risked their lives to be involved in. To just erase someone's entire reasons for what they are doing, and then replace them with something else, is just such an intense form of symbolic violence—to say, "Oh, you moved because you were trafficked," not "Oh, you moved because you had no work, or because you wanted to move. You wanted to live in New York City, just like a lot of other people do, and this is your route." It turns violence into something benevolent.

Ideal Victims and Benevolent Rescuers

FIONA: The image politics are very significant to this understanding of the trafficked subject. It is an image, as you say, of a perfect victim: a young woman forced to sleep with fifty men a night.

NANDITA: The images work because people want to be in the role of the rescuer. We don't want to talk about the source of our world's enormous inequalities. We don't want to talk about what free-market capitalism has done to people in the former Soviet Union. We just want to feel sorry for and rescue this individual woman. The images are almost always of women and children, yet most migrants are still men. But few seem to want to talk about most migrants. They want to talk about a single group of people who are going to make them feel like rescuers. I call the anti-trafficking movement the moral reform arm of the anti-immigrant movement. It is so often seen as progressive, caring, feminist. But it is a close cousin of the nineteenth-century anti–white slave movement and the anti–sex work feminism of that period.

FIONA: Do you see any parallels between the anti-trafficking discourse and the War on Terror discourse?

NANDITA: A key difference between the anti-trafficking discourse and the War on Terror discourse is that the trafficking narrative relies on a victim other than you, whereas the persistent terrorist threat hinges on you being the victim. With both, the fear is of these shady, always male, characters who are going to destroy your society. If you look at it historically, whether it is in the anti–white slave discourse of the nineteenth century, or today's anti-trafficking movement, or the terror fears, men are all Othered. The "evil" always lies outside the realm of the hegemonic male.

Reputable studies, rather than the schlock journalism that frames much of the discussion, have shown again and again that most of the people who smuggle people across borders are small operators. Many of them are friends or family members of the victim, often someone from the migrant's village. They are very far removed from the dominant portrayal of smugglers as symbiotic with organized transnational crime networks. But portraying them as big-time mafia is a way of criminalizing and vilifying the only people in the world who are able to move people across borders without permission. And also, rescuing the female Other reinforces the old racist, Orientalist construction of the male Other. It is ultimately an enormous violence that is done to the women as well.

Fear Nation

FIONA: Much of your work pivots around anti-capitalist and anti-nationalist critiques. You have written about the relationship between fearful nationalism and dangerous migration in the context of neoliberalism and globalization. Can you talk about that?

NANDITA: There has never been a nation-state that has not created a dangerous Other, which is often defined as a threatening foreigner. The foreigner is essential to the existence of the national subject. So the dangerous foreigner fulfills the existence of the national subject. But there is a materiality behind this, too, which is that the dangerous foreigners are often the cheapest people to employ. They are usually the most vulnerable in terms of being able to exercise their own agency against employers. All nationalism is fearful nationalism. All nationalisms are built on a fear of the foreigner. I know that sounds very simplistic, but I've also emphasized that there is a material basis for that fear, which is that since there is always a foreign Other, there is always another mechanism of labour market control. In such a system, employers can look to the state to enforce cheapness and vulnerability. In the US, for example, a fear-mongering discourse of the "illegal" swamping us, destroying our wages, our way of life, and so on is pervasive. This use of fear leads directly to the cheapness of labour. To have the population in the US fearful of undocumented migrants—whether they are thought to be the cause of wage compression, crime, or whatever—it is that fear that makes people cheap and vulnerable. That is the most explicit and clear relationship between nationalism and capitalism. Without that fear, we wouldn't have nation-states, and if we didn't have nation-states, we wouldn't have state control over labour markets.

FIONA: How do you see fear as a technology of power? How is it productive of certain power-effects?

NANDITA: If you look at the discourse of the political right in the US, immigration is one of the few areas, along with prisons, in which it is calling for more state action. The fear is very productive in fostering support for the nation-state, encouraging people to think that we absolutely need this institution and we need it because the borders are out of control. There are a lot of critiques about the state not doing enough, so it's a discourse of betrayal rather than an anti-state discourse, which the right does in every other arena. For the right, the only victim that matters is the national subject. For others, the victim is expansive. The common thread is the designation of the victim. When you recognize whom it is that various movements are designating as the victim, you understand the content of the politics underlying their claims on the figure of the migrant.

FIONA: We've been talking a lot about right-wing preoccupations with danger, fear, and protection. This obsession strikes at the heart of the paradox of national belonging that you have been pointing to throughout our discussion, which is that the nation-state, especially in our era of mass movement and increasingly harsh border controls, is a system of organization that institutionalizes and systematizes differential inclusion. For some, the nation-state is a site of protection and advantage. For others, it is a site of terror and abjection. How do you think through this division of the nation as a protective shield for some and a dangerous place for others?

NANDITA: One thing that is really difficult about analyzing discourses and their hegemonic character is grasping the ways in which they do really work for some people. It does help to be a particular kind of national subject when you're trying to cross the border—an American, Canadian, or EU national subject, versus an Indian, Chinese, or Syrian national subject. So there is something tangible and material about the consequences of these divisions.

To think about these kinds of questions, I always return to Peter Linebaugh and Marcus Rediker's 2000 book *The Many-Headed Hydra*. In particular, I return to the parts where they talk about how practices of controlled mobility were institutionalized and legitimized through the differential allocation of mercy and terror. Today, the national shield, when it is offered and taken up by those who can access it, offers a kind of mercy. People with the right passports can say, "I got to go to Germany with no problem." Every time you get to move like that, the mercy is shown, and the terror continues apace. It is important to pay attention to how it does actually work for certain groups of people at certain times, and that is in part why it can legitimately not work for others. I think that is the most difficult thing to deal with when you are trying to change the system. If it didn't work for anyone, it would be easier to change it.

Love and Fear

FIONA: This makes me think about how love, caring, and intimacy enter into this discussion. Nationalism is often expressed as a kind of love: love of the abstract nation and of abstract people, living and dead, associated with a place. Supposedly, we do not let bad things happen to those we love. In the same way that we are usually conditioned to think about love in terms of scarcity—that there are limits to our love—the border acts as a kind of organizer of the limits of love.

NANDITA: I've been thinking a lot about the scale of society lately. What is the scale of the society that we live in? The more I think about it, the more convinced I am that we live in a global society. I mean this in the sense that the absolutely integral relationships and interdependencies that exist at the level of society are taking place at a global scale. Empires operated at a global scale, far beyond state borders, and that level of cross-state inter-action and interdependency has only increased since the end of various empires. But nation-states continue to control people's mobility, as well as people's empathy for whom they consider to be part of their society.

In a global society, this reliance on hierarchies and exploitation and competition, the control over people's mobility and over their affective ties to one another, are absolutely essential. The way that power is orga-nized today says that you can't have affective ties at a global level. You can't have mobility for human beings at a global level because it would disrupt so much of the way capital derives its profits, and the way that order is maintained in this system. So that relationship between fearful nationalism and capitalism is about limiting who you love. And by exten-sion, everyone you don't love is someone you may advisedly fear. So the love becomes a paranoid one, a jealous one, that says, "I must hang on to what I have, because everyone is trying to get it!" This is essential to how profits are made and order is kept.

FIONA: It is a means by which some people can be cast out as the unloved and unlovable.

NANDITA: Yet remember that there has never been a society made up exclu-sively of citizens. All national societies have had foreigners in them. What do you do with the fact that the unloved are always within? The ideology of the nation-state is that the unloved are always outside, but the reality is that they are inside. And arguably, rather than seeing wars as the state's primary arena of supposedly legitimate coercion, the site where the state gets to use its force legitimately against people is really the Other within.

Arguably, most states expend more resources and ideological energy dealing with the "Other within" than the "Other without," whether it's slaves, the "yellow peril," Indigenous "savages," or women having sex. Think about how much energy is spent on all that fear!

FIONA: It is a kind of infra-imperialism, or imperialism at home, which is presented as protection from the untold dangers lurking therein.

NANDITA: Imperialism at home can never be acknowledged, because the space of society is the nation. For most of us, society is the nation. The distortions undergirding this powerful idea become especially obvious when you are talking about all these unloved people. This is where you find that the distance between rhetoric and reality is especially huge! The nation exists because of all the hatred within it. It continues to exist because there are people designated to be the objects of hate within it.

During the height of anti-war activism in the 2000s, the anti-war movement insisted on making a distinction between a "war at home" and a "war abroad." But why do we persist with this idea that there is some kind of home space and an "out there" space? It is the same war. Even so, this was actually an important political advance. Previously, people tended to talk only about the war "out there." Now, at least, there is a recognition that the war is already at home. But it is still seen as a separate process. If we go back to the idea of society as "global," this distinction becomes even more mystifying. Why are we conceptualizing these as separate processes? They are the same process. The military actions that a state undertakes inside and outside its borders are part of the same project. They are often targeted at groups who are identified in similar ways.

FIONA: What is keeping us trapped in this distorted conceptual universe?

NANDITA: What is distorted is our capacity to imagine where we are and whom we are with. This is what keeps us from having affective ties with everyone else seen to be outside of that space. Historically, different concepts of who constitutes "us" have limited our ability to make transformative changes, whether it was in the case of colonialism or slavery or whatever. I think among the many questions we need to take into account, a key one for our world today is simple: What are the limits to our affection? I think that as long as we continue to believe we live in a national space, we continue to, perhaps inadvertently, limit whom we are with.

Here we can return to Linebaugh and Rediker's account of differentiated allocations of mercy and terror. In this context, mercy is something that is given to you by power. It is not yours to have. Increasingly, I find that making hard distinctions between those who have been terrorized and those who have been given mercy is part of the problem. Why? Because that has been the game of capitalist power: to have us see each other as absolutely separate people, to have those who continue to be terrorized to be resentful and hateful towards those who are given mercy, and those who are given mercy to not identify at all with those who are, or have been, terrorized. While I respect that there are different material realities as a result of the different allocations of mercy and terror, we still have to recognize that the game of power has always been to create separations between people.

FIONA: You've written about how these separations are mystified. Yet the act of pointing out differential oppressions is also about trying to shed new, harsh light on that which is made to be structurally invisible. Thus, in a way, such divisions are called up with the intention of overcoming the violence of separation. Or perhaps it is simply a symptom of the tradition of left-wing melancholy, which is a means by which people reckon with the vast and overwhelming injustices of the world.

NANDITA: Yes, but how we identify at any particular moment is through a set of political conditions. And what we as activists need to do is to create the kind of political conditions that are possible for us to get out of the game that power is playing. Mahmood Mamdani's 2001 study of the Rwandan genocide, *When Victims Become Killers*, does a great job of historicizing the concept of the creation of a "we" as Hutu and as Indigenous to Rwanda. But it was a colonial state category that designated Hutus as Indigenous and the Tutsi as a foreign, alien group. Prior to the creation of these categories by the Belgian colonial state, nothing of the kind existed. The categories were created by a different set of political conditions that were established after colonization, and yet on and on it goes.

You see in this example how we have come to identify ourselves according to how we have been identified, and yet we don't know the difference anymore. I think that is one of the biggest problems we've been encountering in terms of the inability to respond to power. We don't know the difference between identification and subjectivity. We think that how we have been identified is our subjectivity. And this identification is limiting our ability to have the kinds of affective ties with one another that could lead to political conditions that could make it possible to be a greater challenge to established power.

No Borders, Global Democracy

FIONA: You have argued in different places that the contemporary system of border controls constitutes a system of global apartheid. What do you think is the role of the migrant justice and No Borders movements in creating the possibilities for global democracy?

NANDITA: I think the No Borders movement is one of the key movements in the world today. It has the capacity to show us that the society we live in is actually global. I think most other social movements continue to have an imaginary of the nation. The environmental movement has also shown us that we live in a global society, a sentiment found, for example, in the "Chernobyl Is Everywhere!" slogan that resonated around the world in the aftermath of the disaster. The environmental movement emphasized that no one is immune to the actions of other nation-states. That was a big turning point.

Today, people are moving, particularly the most vulnerable people. These are the people states are rendering illegal or turning into foreigners within the spaces they are living and working in—a technique that is starkly revealed in the dramatic expansion of temporary foreign worker programs. It is important to recognize that the origins of the No Borders movement lie in the actions of migrants demanding that they not be made foreigners where they live. The Sans Papiers movement in Paris was a forerunner to contemporary No Borders movements. Although the Sans Papiers were primarily arguing their case within the logic of the nation-state—that people without papers should be recognized as humans within the French state—this act of saying "We are humans here, even without papers" allows us to begin to recognize that society is global. This is one of the major contributions I see from the No Borders movement, which is exciting and unique in some respects. I think that the possibility of recognizing the global-ness of the society we live in ushers in the possibility of expanding affective ties, expanding the definition of who we are, and whom we are with in this world. Any politics that can create conditions of democracy today ought to hold at its core the determination to end the hatred we see directed towards those we fear as terrorists and those we feel sorry for as victims—all these designations, in other words, that separate "us" from "them."

The No Borders movement challenges the politics of fear by showing us that the world is global and that the system of border controls is a system of apartheid in a global society. Only when we see society as global do we have any chance of expanding those affective ties. Otherwise, we are stuck with the same old acts of solidarity or strategic alliances, instead of an active project to remake this society in a democratic way.

FIONA: Do you see in this mass refusal of the border as a technology of fear new openings for the construction of a substantive global society and democracy?

NANDITA: I am not trying to say that migrants are some kind of vanguard of global-ness. But they can show those of us who are not migrants the kind of world that is possible, because they are activating it through their actions. Whoever they are as individuals, when they make the decision to cross a border, especially without official permission, they show us how the border plays a powerful ideological role. They show us how ridiculous our fear of the undocumented border crossers is, because he or she is just another human being. The border crosser is not the employer who is going to cut your wages. The border crosser is just another worker.

It is important to emphasize that it is not just the act of migration that is going to bring about new affective ties. It is the movements that work with migrants that make that a possibility. I am troubled by this tendency I see in certain theories right now to only talk about the migrants and their actions. These are obviously important, but in the absence of a movement that is framing those actions in particular ways, this will have little impact beyond the individual. The anti-immigration movement shows this in reverse, because it frames border crossing as a threat. It politicizes the act of migration in a particular direction. So the migrants themselves are doing things that can be framed in various ways, and the No Borders movement is framing those actions, consciously, as a political act. It is an act that says, "We are humans too," or "The world is global," or "There is a global apartheid." So it is not just the actions themselves that are creating this political consciousness; it is the act of politicizing that migration.

I think the other thing the No Borders movement is good at doing is implicating everyone, not just the migrant we feel sorry for or act in solidarity with, in the concept that we actually live in the same place, the same world, the same society. They are in our society and we are in their society. This is, arguably, the greatest conceptual challenge to state power and to capitalism, because it takes away that game of who becomes the subject of mercy and who is made the object of terror. Ultimately, the No Borders movement is an anti-citizenship project because it is an anti-state project, and, logically, an anti-capitalist project.

5

JOHN HOLLOWAY

We Are the Fragility of the System

JOHN HOLLOWAY is a social theorist and professor of sociology at the Autonomous University of Puebla in Mexico. His work straddles Autonomous Marxism, Frankfurt School–inspired cultural critique, and the political thought of the Zapatistas. His ideas about revolution and social change in our era of recurrent and deepening crisis are propelled by his passionate critique of capitalist rationality. Soon after he moved from Britain to Mexico in the early 1990s, the Zapatista uprising erupted onto the global political stage. From the moment of their appearance, the Zapatistas posed a wholesale reinvention of revolutionary thought and action to a world reeling from twin crises: the collapse of state socialism, and the ascendancy of neoliberalism. Holloway found great inspiration in the Zapatista critique of both the savage destruction wrought by neoliberalism and conventional left theory and practice. Since the uprising began, Holloway has been drawing on the movement's political thought to develop his own influential and widely debated contribution to theories of revolution in the post–Cold War neoliberal era.

Capitalism, Holloway argues, is propelled by a dynamic of attack. It attacks the people upon whom it inescapably relies through acts of enclosure and violence, and the appropriation of human creativity; capital seeks to escape its condition. But people constantly refuse their subordination to capital, and this insubordination is the key to understanding capitalism's recurrent crises. When people refuse their subordination, and moments arise when this refusal becomes unmanageable because it cannot be repressed or reabsorbed into the circuit of domination, capital is thrown into crisis. This, argues Holloway, is the source and nature of the crisis the world is experiencing today. Hence, he urges us to think not about what capital is doing, but about how people are figuring out other ways of creating and acting outside of the capitalist matrix, whether they are farmers distributing their produce directly to consumers in austerity-riven Greece, or Zapatistas building autonomous communities in an increasingly militarized Mexico.

Holloway's critique of state-centric prescriptions for revolutionary change has sparked intense discussion among Marxist scholars and social activists alike. His ideas have been taken up by a number of signal social movements of the last decade, including Argentina's *piqueteros* and South Africa's Shack Dwellers. His book *Change the World without Taking Power* (Pluto Press, 2002) was a major international sensation, provoking passionate, and often fierce, debate among grassroots activists and academics. Holloway further developed the central themes of *Change the World* in his follow-up book *Crack Capitalism* (Pluto Press, 2010). In this interview, we focus on the relationship between fear and fetishism, refusal, debt, and what Holloway has theorized as the all-important search for the inevitable cracks in the architecture of capitalist domination.

Asking We Walk

FIONA: First, I would like to ask if you would start us off with the background story to your writing, thinking, and political engagements. What thoughts and experiences brought you to the ideas you develop and the provocations you raise in *Change the World without Taking Power*?

JOHN: Theoretically, I suppose I come from the Marxist debates about the state that sprang up in Britain in the 1970s. At that time, there was a referendum on the integration of Britain into the European Community. We started with the idea that to understand European integration we had to understand the state, and came to the conclusion—following the German debates on the state at that time—that it was necessary to understand the state as a form of social relations. If we think of the state as a particularly capitalist form of social relations, then there is no way we can think of the transition to a different sort of society as coming about through the state. To say that the state is a capitalist form of social relations is to say that it imposes certain forms of behaviour and thinking and organization upon us. This makes it impossible to break radically with capitalism. So one of the implications of the state is that we have to think of anti-capitalist struggles in terms of anti-state forms of social relations, of language and behaviour, and relating to one another.

This theoretical background came together partly with the anti–poll tax campaign in Britain during the late 1980s and early 1990s. This was a massive movement of disobedience, and it was a pretty imaginative movement in terms of proposing alternative forms of action. After I moved to Mexico, this theoretical orientation came together again. Then, of course, there was the Zapatista uprising in 1994. Zapatistas were saying, and are still saying, that they want to change the world, to make the world anew, but without taking power. So I suppose the Zapatistas are really the important influence behind *Change the World*.

FIONA: Given the quite different debates and forms of social movements, how did you find the move from a European context to a Mexican one?

JOHN: It was very exciting to move to Mexico—to Latin America in general. I think in Europe, and possibly more so in the United States and Canada, being an anti-capitalist is an isolating experience. You are really talking to a small group of people, and you're lucky if you've got anyone to work with at all. You're saying things that just don't make any sense to most of your colleagues and students. Here in Mexico, it is different because of the social situation and the whole tradition of struggle in Latin America, including in the universities. Of course there is still a sense of isolation, but it is not the same at all. There is a completely different echo. It is just so much more obvious that radical change is urgently necessary. So when you're talking about that necessity, people know what you're talking about. Plus, people have the theoretical background and the historical experience. It is very exciting. Latin America is at the forefront of anti-capitalist struggle and real creativity: the Zapatista uprising, the Argentina uprising, Bolivia in the last few years, and so many other experiments are happening all over the place. It is just a moment of enormous creativity and excitement, in spite of everything. All of this is in spite of everything.

Take Guatemala, for example. A couple of years ago I went there to take part in two days of discussion on the question of the state. The participants were a mixture of students, young people from other movements in the city, and young people coming from Indigenous cooperatives set up by ex-guerrillas. These were the children of the guerrillas. It was just so exciting to meet kids who at fourteen were organizing alternative radio programs on the free trade agreement with the US! The age range of the participants was twelve to twenty-nine or so, and that is very hard to imagine happening in the European context.

Dignity against Fear

FIONA: That is impressive. And perhaps the reference to the amazing creativity and courage of so many people in Guatemala, a place filled with people who are trying to recover from four decades of brutal war and a string of military dictatorships, is a good place to turn to the relationship between fear, capitalism, and the state. How do you see the role of fear in capitalist society?

JOHN: I think the issue of fear is very important. Here in Mexico, fear is felt acutely in terms of everyday violence, fear of the police, and so on. That is a constant issue in people's everyday lives.

Thinking of ourselves not as objects but as subjects is crucial. The whole left discourse is just so centred on the notion of ourselves as victims, as objects of capitalist domination, that I think a lot of the time we feel frightened. We frighten ourselves into inactivity. We construct such a picture of this overwhelming system of domination that confronts us and how awful it is, and all that is true. In a sense, it is important to say all that, but if we don't go beyond it, we end up in a position where there is nothing we can do. In a way, I suppose what we are doing is trying to shock ourselves into action. But in fact, we end up frightening ourselves instead. This is one reason it is very important to think of ourselves not as objects but as subjects—as subjects of struggle against our own objectification.

For this, the concept of dignity is absolutely central. Dignity, in the sense that I am talking about it, is not a positive concept. It's not, "I'm a dignified person." That idea often comes with a notion of pompousness. Rather, I am talking about a notion of dignity that is an assertion of my dignity against its negation. In spite of everything, in spite of the society that humiliates me, despite living in a society that turns us into objects, this domination is never entirely complete. In spite of all that, I am still a subject. In spite of all that, I am the starting point; we are the starting point. We are the subjects who create our world. In spite of capital being so awful, we must remember that in the end, we are not entirely dominated. Not only are we not completely dominated, but we are also the ones who actively create. So capital depends on us.

When they rose up in 1994, the Zapatistas started talking about dignity. This is the key concept, they said, and this is why we are rising up. Dignity is what we had forgotten. We were ashamed of having forgotten our dignity, and now we have to redeem the memory of our forefathers and foremothers by remembering our dignity. This seems to be an absolutely fundamental concept. It is a concept that recovers, in spite of everything, a sense of our own subjectivity. It struck me, and probably lots of people, as being kind of a strange concept. But you can see how amazingly potent it has been, because it is echoed over and over again: in Argentina, in Bolivia, in all of the important uprisings of the last decade or so.

Perhaps one way of thinking about fear and anti-fear is in terms of a contrast between a politics of poverty and a politics of dignity. Dignity, for me, seems to be more important in terms of refusing to see ourselves as objects. In a sense, traditional left politics treats us as being the poor. We are the poor victims of capitalism. If we think of ourselves as being the poor, downtrodden victims of capitalism, then we need somebody to lead, to help, to find the way out. If we think in terms of poverty, "poor us" as our starting point, then we're really thinking in terms of hierarchical structures. But we are not so terribly downtrodden. Rather, we are the downtrodden, and therefore we are fighting against this. Then we start not from "poor us," but from "dignified us." We start from our own dignity, and that implies other forms of organization. We don't need leaders if we have dignity. If we have dignity, then the important thing is to develop forms of organization that can recognize that dignity. And this means horizontalism, in the sense of anti-verticalism. It means listening to one another. It means a politics not of monologue, but of dialogue. Or, you could say, a politics of listening rather than a politics of talking. This means seeing ourselves in the context of the council tradition and not the party tradition of anti-capitalism. It means, I suppose, thinking that we are not the objects of fear—that they are the ones who should be afraid of us.

FIONA: And it appears as though they are.

JOHN: They are. Thinking that we are not the objects of fear means, in a sense, turning the world upside down, seeing that capital depends on us, that they are afraid of us. It means recognizing the enormous apparatus they use to maintain the discipline, recognizing the degree to which the day-to-day reproduction of capital requires an enormous army of police. It requires not just state but also private police, and systems of policing within schools, within universities, everywhere. You could see all of that, I suppose, as a measurement of their fear. It is important to turn the whole picture upside down and see that they are afraid of us. They are afraid not just that we might hang them from the nearest lamppost, but also that we might simply not do what they want us to do. Being a boss, I suppose, must be a kind of gamble if you have any sensitivity at all. You tell people what to do without knowing if they're actually going to do it. I suppose this comes across in stories about schools and teachers, when teachers are telling students what to do and wondering if they will.

FIONA: Why do you think the discourse of victimization, rather than the stance of antagonism, is so prevalent in the left tradition?

JOHN: I don't know—partly because it's true. There really is terrible poverty, there really is terrible discrimination, and there really is terrible violence against us. It has a basis; it is just that if you stop there, it seems to me that it becomes destructive, and even comfortable, because you don't have to think about it. You have a kind of scheme of things that is provided in advance. If you think of things in that way, then of course we must struggle to make the world better. But you've already got your model of how to do it. You've got your idea of what revolution is: the party, and your idea of taking power. If you say we have to start not from poverty but from dignity, then you are trying to invent ways forward. The Zapatistas are trying to invent, to create a path by walking.

Fear reduces the person to an idea of the poor as objects, and that actually reproduces, in a sense, a discourse of fear. If you say, "No, that's not the place to start—all that is true, but we have to start not from the poverty of these children who don't have enough to eat, but actually from the dignity of these children," this means you have to rethink change from the standpoint of people's own struggles, from their own refusal to accept that poverty. Then you're really posing the issue in terms of dignity and anti-fear in a way that understands that people confront their own fears, their own objectification. This is really what Zapatismo is all about.

Screaming in the Darkness

FIONA: You launch *Change the World* with a discussion of the scream of refusal of subjugation, which, you argue, resonates everywhere and all the time. Your invocation of the scream is suggestive of a joyful whoop—a refusal and a spontaneous eruption that is also, possibly, a moment of creation. So while the scream suggests fear, it is also a creative articulation. Could the metaphor of the scream be useful for thinking about the dynamics of hope and fear, or revolution and subordination?

JOHN: I think of the scream as being a scream of horror and of rage. It is both the scream of the victim and the refusal to be a victim. It is the scream of somebody who is terrified and refuses to just live with that terror. I suppose if you're terrified, there are two things you can do: hide your head in your hands and hope that nobody will notice you, or give expression to that terror in the scream. The scream is already a response to terror. It is really saying, "I refuse to be terrified." It is a scream that comes out of the dark and refuses to accept the dark. Lots of times, it seems there is no way forward. Really, there's very little hope for humanity; we're destroying ourselves at breathtaking speed, literally and completely annihilating humanity. And precisely because the situation is so terrifying, it becomes all the more important to scream and find a way forward.

Thinking through Crisis

JOHN: I think that has a lot to do with thinking of the world from the perspective of crisis. What we are really looking for is hope, for cracks, and trying to think about the world from the standpoint of its fragility. This means trying to understand domination as a system of domination in crisis. That is the importance of Marxism. Marxism sees history as a system. It is not a period of domination; it is really a period of crisis in domination. For me, that is what distinguishes Marxism from other forms of left thought, which are very good indeed at throwing light on domination. Feminism, for example, showed just how all-pervasive patriarchal domination is. Ecological thought has shown just how terrible the destruction of nature is. But they don't, at least as far as I know, really focus on the fragility of domination, whereas I think that Marxism, at least the way I understand it, really takes the crisis of domination as a central question.

For this reason, Marxism urges us to recognize that we ourselves are that fragility. Because that is really our question. The key question is not really how we understand the fragility of the system outside. It is: How do we understand that we ourselves are the fragility of the system, that we are the crisis of the system? So it is crucial to understand the crisis not in terms of objective laws, but in terms of the force of our own struggle.

To bring this back to the question of fear, I suppose that means understanding domination as being something that is in constant crisis. We are in constant crisis, and therefore the dominators are in constant fear and terror. They express it from time to time, although not very often. But they do have a whole apparatus of thought that tries to contain that terror of their fragility, the fear of their own fragility. One book that brings that out particularly is Tom Wolfe's *The Bonfire of the Vanities*. The ruling classes behind their high walls are living in terror. You feel that more and more every day. In Mexico you see more and more people living behind high walls with guards and controls, and that seems to be the trend throughout the world.

FIONA: Are we moving closer to an ever more enhanced version of Hobbes's infamous state, where adherence to the sovereign is attained through the mobilization of fearful passions?

JOHN: Yes, I suppose if we think of it in those terms, the state is really the expression of the antidote to the ruling classes' fear. Obviously Hobbes puts it in very general terms, and you could read it that way. If you think of the ruling classes or simply the rich as living in constant fear, the state is their way of dealing with that. From that point of view, you can perhaps see the state as being a process of inverting fear, of turning fear around by trying to make the people they are afraid of live in fear. That is what happens. We have a "who is afraid of whom" situation, which means everybody is afraid of everybody else.

Living in the Subjunctive

FIONA: Let's continue on the trail of the scream, but turn it towards your reflections on language and communication. You argue for both world revolution and an approach to it that means living in the subjunctive, by which you seem to mean living in a way that recognizes that one cannot know in advance the outcome of one's struggle. To this end, you emphasize the importance of asking questions and not knowing, and draw on the writings of the Zapatistas, especially the movement's all-important phrases, like *caminamos preguntando* (asking we walk). I'm interested to hear about your thoughts on language and its role in building new forms of subjectivity. How do you see the relationship between language and emancipation?

JOHN: If you think of experiencing fear as being helpless, a feeling of help-lessness can be seen, I suppose, as having a lot to do with fetishism, in the sense that the social relations of capitalism construct the world of things and the world that we don't control. In that sense, fetishism implies our own objectification, our own feeling of helplessness. It implies that we are de-subjectified, that we are confronted with a world of alien objects—things that we are afraid of, whether we call them God or gods, or whether we call them money or the state. This means that we are deprived of our own subjectivity, our own activity, our own doing. In that sense, we are confronted by a world of nouns: nouns as the expression of things, nouns as the linguistic construct that expresses the closure of our own activity. The noun excludes our doing. It excludes our own creating.

FIONA: Because it is a completion?

JOHN: Yes, because it is a completion, a closure, a result of a past action, something that is outside of us. So to recover our own subjectivity, our own doing and creating, means a revolt of verbs against nouns. A revolt of doing against the world of things.

FIONA: One thing you mention in *Change the World* is how liberating and how terrifying it would be to actually live a life in verbs instead of our habit of living in a world of nouns—how exciting and scary that would be, because it would signal a life of permanent action, which is an interesting way to think about the materiality of language.

JOHN: I think it implies a life of intensity that we would find difficult to cope with. But that is because we are who we are. We are the cripples created by capitalism. To live at that degree of intensity would be amazing and amazingly frightening.

FIONA: It would. And why is this intensity akin to living in the subjunctive tense, as you say?

JOHN: I think its importance lies partly in the way it is suggestive of uncertainty. In a way, we kind of live beneath the surface. Our struggles always come from invisibility. Visibility is an expression of power. And the struggle against power relations is to rise up from that which is repressed. A movement that comes from below comes from a repressed world. So in that sense, it is always a movement against invisibility. The rising up of an invisible world. This is made very clear if you think of the feminist movement or the Indigenous movement. If you think of the Zapatista symbol of the balaclava, it conveys this idea: by making ourselves invisible, we rise up against our real invisibility. They are saying that by showing the way we are invisible, we make you look at us. You could say the same thing about the gay rights movement, as well. It is a movement against the invisibility of a certain form of sexual activity that is made invisible.

So, in a sense, it is subjunctive because it is the language of the subterranean movement. These movements are structurally subterranean because that is what power means: pushing things beneath the surface, so that there is a sense of protest or anti-capitalism as being always close to madness. It is not only that we seem mad to other people, but that we at times feel that maybe we ourselves are mad—maybe this is just crazy. I think we have to accept this, in a way; we have to assume that we will have to take this feeling on board.

FIONA: I'm curious because the subjunctive is rather buried in the English language. I wonder if over the course of developing a culture so infused with a commercial, transactional orientation, the language itself has buried the subjunctive aspects of its sensibility. Further, the subjunctive, or the ambiguous dimension of speech, is a verb form. In your critique of fetishism, you talk about the importance of thinking about the world and social change in terms of verbs, rather than the more closed, noun-oriented interpretation that stunts our political imaginations.

JOHN: I suppose there is a sense that the use of nouns is part of the process of fetishism, of the way in which capitalism comes to be seen as a closed system, something that *is*. Conventionally, that is what revolution is about: the destruction of this capitalism that is. I think the left takes that on and completely reproduces it. Whereas, if you begin to think in terms of verbs, of processes, you can see that capitalism is something that we produce or reproduce all the time. You see that if capitalism exists, it exists because we are making it exist. If it exists today, it is not because somebody created it in the eighteenth to nineteenth century, but because we today are creating it. And then that means that the question of changing the world is not so much a question of destroying capitalism but refusing to create it.

The problem is, how can we stop creating this dreadful system? If we know that capitalism won't exist tomorrow if we don't create it, how can we take action to stop creating capitalism tomorrow? Then you think of revolution in a different way. You can focus on new questions, about what we can do, and that actually helps us to see the power of what we are doing or not doing. Because it is not that we are helplessly banging our heads against the wall: we are actually creating or not creating the capitalist system. It is not that the system is there and we are hurling ourselves against it. That is what we feel, that we are hurling ourselves against this terrible, terrible, immovable system. But in fact, it is not true. It is actually that we are creating the system and hurling ourselves against it at the same time, which then means thinking in terms of the dual and antagonistic character of our own activity.

Fear's Antagonists

FIONA: Can you elaborate on this idea of our dual and antagonistic character?
JOHN: One thing that Marx says at the beginning of *Capital*, something that is absolutely, completely overlooked, is that the dual character of labour is the key to understanding everything. I suppose that is what I am very much hung up on at the moment. I think a part of overcoming fear, or overcoming fetishism, is to try and understand the world in terms of our own doing. Part of overcoming nouns is trying to understand the world in terms of our own doing. We create this awful world. We also struggle against it. It means trying to understand in terms of the antagonistic nature of what we ourselves do.

We as university teachers actually actively create systems of authority, verticality and fear, qualification and disqualification, on the one hand. But, on the other hand, if we are critical, we also struggle against it. We are doing both at the same time. And socially, we as collective humanity are creating the system that is destroying us and struggling against it at the same time. We are creating a structure of fear and helplessness on the one hand, and on the other hand we are struggling against it.

How do we understand the relationship between these two types of activity? We understand capitalism in terms of the dual character of our doing, the dual character of our labour. And, to come back to the question of crisis, we have to understand the crisis of the capitalist system in terms of the antagonistic nature of these two dimensions of activity. Marx talks about it in terms of contradiction, in terms of the duality of abstract labour and concrete labour. Putting it in those terms, we need to understand the crisis of capital in terms of the crisis of abstract labour, or the crisis of the labour that creates capital. The central social antagonism is not between labour and capital, as Marxists tend to say. For Marx, the central antagonism was between abstract labour and the kind of potentially free activity that is contained, or not contained, within abstract labour. Think of the crisis of capitalism as a crisis of labour.

FIONA: Would you say that activity that is free and not free at the same time is the kernel of the crisis? From where do you imagine that crisis emerging, or turning into a verb, as you might say?

JOHN: I think that it is there all the time. I think it comes into sharp focus in certain periods.

FIONA: This makes me think of your discussion of the politics of events and how they open possibilities, create cracks or openings. How do those moments of opening expand into different forms of connection or solidarity?

JOHN: Coming back to the question of fear, if we think of capitalism as a kind of system of fear and helplessness—helplessness because as a system of objectification of people, it makes them helpless—then I see the cracks in terms of spaces or moments in which we assert our own subjectivity. Cracks occur when we assert our own refusal to be afraid, our refusal to be helpless. There are moments or spaces in which we say, "No, we are not going to be the objects of capitalist command. We shall do what we consider to be necessary or desirable. We are not going to be nouns, we are going to be verbs." And one obvious example would be the Zapatista saying "*Ya Basta* [Enough]!", by which they are saying, "Enough! We are not going to carry on being the objects of humiliation, the objects of domination anymore. We are going to create our own world." That is what they've been struggling to do over the years.

But these cracks also operate very much on the individual level, like when you say, "Today I won't go to work, because what is important to me is to stay at home and play with my children, or stay in bed with my lover," or whatever. Of course, this is not the same thing as organizing an uprising in Chiapas. It isn't. There are real differences. But if we don't see lines of continuity between the two, then we isolate ourselves. We create a ghetto for ourselves. I think that is what the left does all the time. We say that the Zapatista uprising is something we have to take seriously, that it is politically important, whereas staying in bed for the day is reactionary and frivolous. That seems to be a great mistake, because if we don't actually draw a line of continuity from one type of crack to another type of crack, we are cutting off the possibility of the crack spreading.

The idea of the crack is not just an autonomous space; it's a space of autonomy and movement. Cracks spread; they join up or they don't join up. They expand, they get filled up. If we say that the only serious cracks are the big cracks, the politically conscious, organized cracks, we are actually closing off the possibility of cracks spreading and making contact with the smaller cracks. And one thing that is absolutely brilliant about the Zapatistas, especially in the early days, is their capacity to make connections with smaller cracks, or cracks that are experienced individually.

And I suppose that is the point you were making by talking about anti-fear earlier. You were making links between the very deep, personal experience of fear on the one hand, and a major political issue on the other hand. You are drawing these lines of continuity. And on the left we have this terrible tendency to say, "No, we won't accept these lines of continuity." That seems to be really, really dangerous.

Resonances

FIONA: I think one of the most inspiring and politically attuned examples of the Zapatistas in this regard, especially, as you say, in the early days, is their persistent invocation of housewives as political subjects. They always included housewives in their open pantheon of important political subjects and actors. It is so different from our conventional political language that it is almost unrecognizable. I think that's why so many people on the electoral and vanguardist left were so scandalized by the Zapatistas. The subjects were so difficult for them to recognize.

JOHN: That's right, absolutely. There is a tendency to divide the Zapatista discourse into the serious and the poetic, to see the jokes and irreverent speech as just adornments, when in fact they are precisely the opposite. The question of resonance is so important here. How do we resonate with the anti-capitalism that is inside all of us—inevitably inside all of us simply because of the fact that we live in capitalism, we live in an oppressive society, a society that oppresses and represses? Some sort of reaction against that repression is inevitable. The question is: How do we make contact with that anti-capitalism, instead of dismissing it? Rather than saying, "Oh, they're just integrated into the system," or "They're just petit bourgeois," how do we bring to life these lines of continuity? The theme of fear and anti-fear seems to be very powerful because it cuts through and makes those contacts. It is actually something that touches everything and everybody. I suppose anti-fear is not a question of being courageous. It is more a matter of saying, "Well, living in this society, there is no way that we cannot experience fear." There is no way that we cannot be sexist and racist. It is not a question of non-sexist, non-racist, and non-afraid. It is a question of being anti-sexist, anti-racist, and anti-afraid.

FIONA: It is not to say that you should be this or you should be that, or that you're not brave enough. But to think about fear in terms of refusal is to think about it in terms of hope.

JOHN: I hadn't thought about it in relation to hope. I suppose anti-fear is another way of expressing hope, but, as you say, starting from negation. Making the connection between fear and hopelessness or fear and despair, in a sense. I suppose it is also the notion of hope against hope. Thinking of hope not just as a positive category, but as a negative one.

Against and Beyond

JOHN: I tend to think of struggle as struggle against and beyond. In other words, the starting point is always "against." To become really forceful, the scream or the "no" must become not just an "against," but an "against and beyond," in which we try to do things that go beyond the capitalist social relations that we are saying "no" to. I suppose if you just say "no" to capital, how do you go beyond that? How do you survive? Whereas if you say "no," but also say that we can create different social relations and different forms of living ourselves, then that is a much more powerful "no."

For example, think of workers saying "no" to their employers. If they just go on strike, they are in a way saying, "No, we won't accept your domination under these particular conditions. But if you change your conditions, the offer of wages or whatever, then we will accept." Whereas if the workers don't just go on strike, but actually take over the factory and show that they can do other things with their skills, equipment, and so on, it's a more fundamental challenge, because it's pushing against and beyond. It's saying, "Not only can we say 'no,' but we can actually create things that break through such social relations."

I think the struggle is really a struggle against and beyond, a struggle that tries to create a here and now of different social relations, a struggle that tries to create the world for which we are struggling. I think that has been a feature of struggles particularly over the last two decades. There is a sense that it can't be a question of building for the future; there is an emergency and we have to create different social relations here and now, and we have to do things in a different way. So the Zapatistas, to come back to them, are not just demanding other conditions; they are creating that here and now, without asking permission. I think that has been a very important feature of movements all over the place: the idea that we have to create that here and now. We have to create the world we want. And the way we relate to one another here and now, the way that we act and the way we organize—we can't reproduce the patterns of capitalism. We have to create the otherness for which we are struggling.

FIONA: The otherness?

JOHN: Yes, the other world.

This is obviously extremely difficult. What does it mean to really create different social relations within capitalism? How can we really break with this system? Can we really create something that goes beyond this system? I think this is really the difficult point of conflict. On the one hand, yes, that is what we are doing, with all these autonomous groups and different forms of struggle. On the other hand, it is always contradictory. It always confronts very severe problems, whether in the form of state repression or state co-optation. But I think we have to think of the struggle as against and beyond. In that sense, yes, it is very creative. We are creating something else at the same time as we necessarily talk about the problems involved.

Think of Argentina, for example. There was very much a feeling among people, particularly during the uprising of 2001, that through our actions, through our movements, through our groups, we were creating a different world. We were doing things in a different way. Now, years later, the problems are much clearer. The same goes for the Zapatistas. They really are creating a different world within their own communities, and through movements throughout Mexico. But this is also very problematic, so it is important to say both things. On the one hand, it is important to say, "This refusal is really happening; it is really fundamental and important, really wonderful," and also to say that it is really problematic, that it really comes up against the severe problems of how we learn from those experiences. We tend to forget the wonderfulness, and just talk about the problems. I don't think it's right. Nor is it right to forget about the difficulties and just celebrate the wonderfulness, because you begin to take off into a non-real world. That really doesn't help. To focus on only the good or the bad is problematic, and it is important to retain a sense of reality through self-critique.

FIONA: I suppose one problem we are constantly confronted with is the ever more sophisticated elaboration of both bald repression and absorption into the dominant practice that always confronts every emancipatory moment, big or small.

JOHN: Yes, a combination of both, and with different balances in different places. In Argentina, following the popular revolt in 2001, the co-optation or absorption has been particularly powerful. In the United States or in Mexico, repression is much more obvious.

FIONA: Fear, then, is difficult to grapple with because it stops the verb from being able to realize itself. A retreat happens. I would like to hear your thoughts on how we could think beyond a discourse of individual courage and towards one of solidarity and collectivity. But there are endless examples of extremely vulnerable people overcoming their fear in all kinds of creative ways when they face repression. For example, when the Guatemalan Women's Sector was attacked and threatened, they held a street party.

JOHN: This makes me think about the question of laughter and just how important clowns have become around the globalization struggles. I attended the anti-G8 events in Rostock, Germany, where I encountered two distinct ways of thinking about how to respond to state violence. The big march was flanked by a massive, very heavily armed police presence, about sixteen thousand police, lined up all along the route. There were two kinds of responses to this. On the one hand, there were the clowns, who would go up to the police and start dancing around, imitating them, giving them flowers, and in some cases making them laugh. That seemed to me a terrific way of de-fetishizing the police. And also of saying, very clearly, that what we were doing was absolutely asymmetrical to what they were doing. Brilliant! And presumably for the clowns themselves, it was a process of confronting personal fear. Dancing around heavily armed police takes a lot of courage. So there is that response. But there was also a massive Black Bloc presence, about four or five thousand. From the start, they were obviously prepared for a confrontation with the police. Many participants were upset because they saw those actions as undermining the broader action.

But there you have two different ways of confronting fear. We had a pretty good discussion about it afterwards, with people involved in the Black Bloc action and others. The Black Bloc people had two completely different explanations. One was to say, "Well, it doesn't matter what most people think or how they act, because they're integrated into the system, so who cares what they think? The way to confront capital is to take on the police first of all, take on parliament, and then take on the capitalists themselves." But the other reaction was much more interesting. It said, "You know, confronting the police is a way of confronting power, empowering ourselves, and confronting our fears. It is a bit like occupying an empty house; we're actually showing people that you can confront power. You can do things that you may feel afraid to do." So there were two different responses to how you deal with this massive presence of police, this reality of state violence.

What struck me very much was the question of symmetry—the question of the asymmetry of the clowns. What shocked me about the Black Bloc was the symmetry of the response. Too many aggressive males against aggressive males, acting according to a preplanned scheme. We knew there was going to be violence. The two sides were prepared for it.

FIONA: At the protests against the G20 in Philadelphia in 2009, the clowns appeared and staged a wonderful piece of political theatre: they turned on one another, announcing that they would attack each other so the police wouldn't have to. Doing this seemed to really challenge the predictable and, as you say, symmetrical relationship between protester and authority, and turning it upside down by making fun of it all.

JOHN: Going back to our "against and beyond" discussion, I suppose you can see the clowns as an against and beyond that is really creative. Through their actions, they are saying, "We are not just going to reproduce the same dynamic. We're going to create new things," whereas the Black Bloc appears to be only against. Without wanting to condemn them, I feel that this is a much less fruitful form of action.

Dignity

FIONA: I'd like to return to the concept of dignity for a moment. Dignity is a central theme in your writing, and especially your writing on the Zapatistas. What do you see as the relationship between dignity and anti-capitalism?

JOHN: Obviously dignity has been there from the beginning of class domination, but I think there is something novel happening today that is encapsulated in the concept of dignity. It is not just that Zapatistas started to use the concept of dignity. I think the concept has something to do with the way in which struggles are changing. These changes have to do with two things. One is the breakdown of the crisis of the Leninist model of revolution, which really created workers as objects, masses that needed to be led. So that is a crisis. Second, I think it is also partly a crisis of time itself: there is a new sense of urgency. Now we have this idea that we cannot think of revolution as something that may happen in fifty years' time, because we do not know if there is going to be much left of humanity in fifty years.

I think there is a sense that people are thinking about change here and now, however difficult or experimental that may be. The idea of change here and now has a lot to do with dignity. Dignity, for me, is the idea that here and now we are subjects and so we must assume our own subjectivity. It is the assumption of our own subjectivity. It is saying "no" to being objectified. Saying a "no" that goes beyond "no." It is a negation and a creation. Again, thinking of the Zapatistas, they are not just saying "no" to the Mexican government. They are saying, "No, and furthermore we are creating our own communities, our own system of autonomies based on the principle of dignity, based on mutual respect," and so on. In that sense, you can talk about dignity if you understand it as negation and creation.

Fear and Debt

FIONA: Throughout our conversation, you have touched on a theme that is also one of the key insights in *Change the World*: your ideas about what you refer to as the fragility of oppression. Would you explain more specifically or concretely what you mean by the fragility of oppression?

JOHN: I think it is partly just to realize that those who dominate always depend upon on those who are dominated. There is always the fear that those who are dominated may suddenly realize that domination is dependent upon the dominated. So there is a whole system of domination that is built upon the containment or control of that fear.

Something that seems very important to the question of fear and the
question of the fragility of domination, and that is specific to this historical period, is the question of debt. I think that capitalism depends more
and more on the expansion of debt, or the expansion of credit, and that
is really the way it has survived or expanded, especially since the Second
World War. This expansion was justified, of course, in terms of Keynes-
ian economic policy. But even with the turn against Keynesianism in
the mid-1970s, when monetarism attacked debt or credit-based expansion, it never succeeded. So capitalism depends more and more on this
constant expansion of debt. And that means, on the one hand, the tremendous fragility of the whole financial system. The present system of
financial management is really designed to avoid the financial upheavals
that are so inherent in any system that is so heavily dependent upon debt.

On the other hand, it also means a huge amount of fear of violence,
because any system of debt is built upon the threat of violence. If I lend
you money, built into that relation is the threat of enforcement. Not
between friends, but certainly if I lend money to somebody in a commercial transaction, it has to be backed by some sort of threat of enforcement.
On the other side of that relationship is the fear of enforcement. Every
time a house is repossessed or whatever, that fear and that threat are made
very real. You can actually build a whole structure of fear deep into society. Think, for example, of strikes. One of the problems of the strike is
people's fear of how they are going to pay their mortgage. In Britain, during the miners' strike in 1985, it was very significant that the first thing
the miners' union did was to negotiate the suspension of mortgage pay-
ments with the building societies during the strike. And they managed to
impose that.

So I think that in thinking of fear and anti-fear, the question of debt is
important. It applies to the fragility of the whole system, and ultimately
to the expression of our own power, because the expansion of credit and
the expansion of debt is a way of trying to contain social conflict. In the
hope that it never happens, it says, "We'll let you live in reasonable conditions; you can borrow the money to have your house, your car, and your
children's education. You don't have to revolt, but you will have to pay

for it." So it means building into people's lives a structure of indebtedness along with the fear of not being able to pay for it—fear of the consequences.

FIONA: Do you see the debt system as a possible crack? It is a contradictory situation; how do contradictions and cracks connect?

JOHN: I haven't thought about it in those terms. But you're right. In that sense, it is seeing the way in which our refusal and our struggles become reflected as apparently separate contradictions within the system. So if you see the expansion of debt and credit as a reflection of the strength of the anti-capitalist movement or the working-class movement, then yes, it would be reflected and apparent in system-immanent cracks.

PART III

PRACTICING

6

LYDIA CACHO

Dangerous Journalism

FEMINIST WRITER and anti-violence activist Lydia Cacho is one of Mexico's most prominent investigative journalists. She is also a public figure renowned for her political courage. In recent years, as Mexico's "war on drugs" has escalated and social violence soared, journalism has become an increasingly dangerous vocation in that country. Like many journalists, Cacho has received numerous death threats over the years, frequently backed up by direct attacks.

While she has investigated several internationally known cases, such as the ongoing murders of women in Ciudad Juarez, much of Cacho's work has taken place in the tourist mecca of Cancun, the city where she has lived for the last two decades. Her reporting on human rights violations and violence against women drove Cacho to establish the city's first shelter for battered women. Over the past two decades, Cacho has focused her energies on issues of violence against and sexual abuse of women and children, and her writing stands out for its particular attention to the impunity enjoyed by Mexico's elite. Following the publication of her 2004 book *Los demonios del Edén* (literally *The Demons of Eden*), an exposé of a Cancun-based pedophile ring, Cacho launched a formal case against some of the most powerful men in Mexico, accusing them of systematic sexual abuse of children for profit. The trial drew enormous public attention, and Cacho endeavoured to use it as a public platform to engage in a wider societal discussion about institutionalized misogyny and generalized impunity in Mexico.

Cacho's journalism has won numerous prizes, including the Civil Courage Prize and the World Press Freedom Hero award of 2010.

Journeys in Lost Cities

FIONA: To begin, I'd like to ask you to tell me about yourself and the experiences and ideas that have influenced your thinking and writing, as well as your life of intense political agitation.

LYDIA: I truly am the product of the women who came before me. My grandparents were intensely involved in politics in Portugal, France, and Spain. They were involved in what we would now call human rights work. My mother was born in France and came to Mexico when she was a girl, and then she met a Mexican guy—my father—and they married. I grew up middle class in Mexico City with a feminist mother, who was also a psychologist and a sexologist. My father was an engineer from a military family. So we had these two worlds in one house, which was incredible to learn from. My grandfather was very important to me. He was born in Portugal into a poor family that was really involved in helping others. He was always looking for ways to connect to others. He loved poetry, and he used to read it to me when I was a little girl so I would learn Portuguese. Those were the basic influences in my life when I was a little girl.

One thing really set me off as a human rights activist. When I was a little girl, my mom used to go to the poor areas of Mexico City. Today they have names and are well-known parts of the city, but back then it was the garbage dump. They were called *ciudades perdidas* (lost cities). The name meant a lot to me because, I thought, "How can you go to a city that is lost?" My mom would go there with her friends, psychologists, sociologists, and activists, and talk with the women about their rights. To do that, they needed to keep their kids busy, so they took my sisters and brothers and me to entertain them. I was very little, and I started asking questions about the conditions the kids were living in. Sometimes I think that might have been too much for children our age.

It was hard, in the sense that they were kids who looked just like me, and they had no chance of getting out of their bleak situation. It was quite painful, and I was too little to understand. I truly suffered from that, and sometimes I would just tell my mom that it was too much and that it was very cruel to bring us so close to that reality. On the other hand, it was an experience that made me who I am. I remember trying to teach a boy around seven or eight how to write and draw. I had a piece of paper and had brought my drawing pencils, but he couldn't hold the pencil. I was shocked that a boy my age couldn't hold a pencil. I couldn't understand that he was so malnourished he didn't have the strength. I remember asking my mom, "How come he cannot write? Why doesn't he go to school? Is he ever going to go to school? Can I give him my license and he can go instead of me?" And my mom said, "No, this is the life he's living, and you have to know this, because one day you will have the chance to act on this. And you have to learn that there is very little that you can do as a person by yourself." My mom used to tell us to cup our hands together and say, "You can only do what is in your hands," and I would say, "But my hands are really tiny," and she'd say, "Well, you do what you can and you learn to ask others to join with you so that you can do more." That's the sort of thing she would tell us all the time.

I grew up being a human rights activist without really knowing it. I didn't decide I was going to do this work. It was just part of my life. That is the way I act as a citizen of my country. I do take care of myself. I read a lot. I became a professional in certain areas that interest me. I became a journalist because that's a profession that I love. I'm good at writing and listening to people. I just knew I was a feminist from the time I was twelve, thirteen, or fourteen years old—whenever was the first time somebody said a really sexist thing to me. Once I tried to confront these kids at school and I had a really bad time. I went back home and talked to my mom, and she said, "Well, you never negotiate your dignity for anything. If you lose friends, that's okay, but you never negotiate your dignity." It just made sense to me.

My father, in a sense, was a macho. He was a cultivated macho, so he never exercised violence against us, but he was violent inside; it came out in the way he talked about certain issues. There were these ongoing discussions. My mom would teach my brothers to cook, and she would take us girls to fix the car. My father would say, "Oh my God, you're going to make them sissies!" to which my mom would say, "There's no such thing!" When I was nineteen I went to Paris to live and stayed there for a little over a year. I wanted to be a journalist. I wanted to be a writer, and I was a feminist. I met people from all over—from Poland, people escaping really tough times, and from countries like Vietnam. I just knew that this was for me. I just sort of promised myself that I would be loyal to myself.

When I went back to Mexico, I was drawn to Cancun to scuba dive. I love the ocean. I wanted to become a poet and write novels and do cultural journalism. But, well, my feminist side came out and I started doing what I had to do there. So I've been a journalist for eighteen years, specializing in what they call human rights journalism. I've written a book of poetry, a novel, and two books of investigative journalism. Twenty years ago I founded Cancun's first shelter for HIV-positive people, and it's still working. Then I moved into issues of violence against women, and I founded a high-security shelter for women in Cancun.

Impunity

FIONA: What does a high-security shelter mean in light of the state of law and justice in Mexico today?

LYDIA: It means batterers cannot get into the house. When a woman is being battered and calls for help, the police are afraid, not only of the husband, but also of being sued for trespassing. Some batterers have sued the police. The law has since changed, but the police still don't want to get involved. Usually in Mexico when you call the police, they get there an hour or two after you call them, so it's not as though it is a safe thing to call the police. When we opened the shelter, we understood that in Mexico the criminal justice system is not just problematic; it's actually useless. If the police are not going to show up when a woman needs help, we need to help her. By the time we opened the shelter, I had already had two or three batterers put a gun to my head. I didn't know what to do, but I managed to talk my way out of it. We needed and wanted to understand what to do! If we were going to go and help women when they called, we needed to create a model for our actions. Our first rule is that we are not violent, so we will not accept violence. But we did need to learn how to protect ourselves and the women. We took judo classes. We learned how to disarm a man and to immobilize someone who is being violent.

The women trusted us, and we would do everything in our hands to protect them from everybody—including the police or a judge—who wanted them back with their husbands. So we built our own shelter. It was a wonderful thing. It's like a place to hide from a hurricane. We have a yoga place and we have gardens in the centre, where the families cultivate flowers and food. On the inside the house is beautiful, but on the outside it is surrounded by barbed wire. Cameras tape everything twenty-four hours a day. We train the women. We don't use guns. We have a three-door pass before you get to the shelter. It's in a secret location, far away from our crisis centre. We change our phones constantly so they cannot be tapped. We use radios, and we change our radio system regularly so the police can't tap into our radio. We have a fairly organized system of high security. Once a woman enters the shelter, we teach her the security plan.

Some of the women who have fled to the shelter are the wives of drug dealers—important, powerful drug dealers. Some of them are the wives or daughters of politicians, or powerful mafia guys. In our system, no woman has ever been harmed. There have been a couple of experiences where drug dealers, with long guns and big guards, have come to the crisis centre and threatened us. In one case, they threatened to kill us and called out my name. That was the first case in which we agreed to press charges against a drug dealer, because it was the only way that we could get the woman access to international asylum. The criminal justice system in Mexico is pretty much like the Canadian system in that it is centred on protecting the group and not the victim. It's centred on imprisonment, but never on making sure the lives of victims are restored. The last study on corruption in the justice system in Mexico demonstrated that out of every one hundred crimes, only two will result in convictions. This means that 98 per cent of the time, criminals get away with whatever. Murder, abduction, family violence, femicide, rape, and everything else.

A Functional Dictatorship

FIONA: How do you think that works in terms of creating a climate of fear, both among the women you work with directly and the general public? You have talked about how this impunity has created a sense of internalized helplessness among people in Mexico right now. How does this affect battered women?

LYDIA: It is linked to the fact that Mexico, as a colonized country, has experienced this feeling for centuries—that nothing belongs to us, that we are not the owners of our lives, of our territory, of our ideas, even. First the Spanish came to Mexico, took everything, and tried to erase who we were. And I think this is important in the cultural context, because they did erase almost everything, but they didn't erase people's notion of being conquered by others. The Spaniards brought their ideas of law and justice, and we cannot forget that the justice system in Spain was already totally corrupt. Along came a horde of ignorant guys with their corrupt justice system to colonize Mexico.

Carlos Fuentes has a wonderful essay explaining the history of corruption in Mexico. He explains that for centuries, the Spanish Viceroyalty drew Mexico from Spain. The guys implementing the law in Mexico were military types who didn't know anything about law or justice. They were ignorant themselves. They ruled Mexico as if it were Spain. At a certain time they had thousands and thousands of rules that had to be followed, and these rules had to do with ridiculous stuff. They brought all these laws to Mexico that made no sense in our reality. And people learned how to get away with breaking all these laws that had nothing to do with them. So colonization imposed this justice system that had nothing to do with reality, and the people created an alternative reality that had nothing to do with law. Corruption was implemented by all of society. Everyone was looking for ways to break the rules, because they were unbelievably ridiculous. Nobody could follow those rules.

So there is a cultural aspect regarding corruption that is quite interesting. Social corruption, with police, the military, everywhere. On top of that we have the PRI [Partido Revolucionario Institucional, or Institutional Revolutionary Party], the party that came to power and stayed for over seventy years. So we have a dictatorship, but it was such an intelligent and soft dictatorship that we can't call it that, because in the eyes of the rest of the world it was sort of a functional government.

FIONA: Progressive, even, with its official discourse of solidarity, social justice, and so forth.

LYDIA: Yes, of course. What happened with Mexican society over seventy years was that a very small group of probably three hundred men have been controlling the whole country. In some states in Mexico, there is a bigger penalty for stealing a cow than for killing a woman or raping a woman. This is not what surprises people. What is surprising is that a judge, in the twenty-first century, would implement that law. He would punish someone for taking a cow and refuse to punish someone for raping a woman because the woman was wearing a miniskirt, for example.

So we have a corrupted society in which we found ways to get away with stuff in order to lead a regular life. And then on top of that we have a seventy-year dictatorship in which the government told us how to behave, how to be. The government controlled the media completely. The president was also the owner of Supreme Court judges, and the president would order them around. Supreme Court judges are in power for fifteen years and they earn high salaries in Mexico, and if you want to stay there you better obey the president. So, on the one hand you had social movements—the feminists, so powerful in the sixties and seventies, and the '68 movement of students. These movements worked with movements throughout Latin America, in El Salvador, Guatemala, Chile, and Argentina. But then on the other hand you had a government that was a dictatorship, but was protected by all these other countries because it didn't look like a dictatorship. Our presidents were never like [former Chilean dictator Augusto] Pinochet. What was really clever about the PRI was that instead of one guy staying forever as president, as they did before winning the revolution, there was a regular rotation of who was visibly in power. One president would serve for six years, but before finishing they would perform the *dedazo*, which means the president would assign the presidency to his successor. That is why it is so hard for people to understand that although we had so many presidents, in practice it was like having only one. Each president followed the rules they were assigned by the others who came before, covering up all their corruption and ensuring impunity for all the things the government did before.

This climate is hard for us, for the social movements, because we're living in a reality that has nothing to do with the image the Mexican government has created around the world for seventy-something years. And that links to corruption and to the strong *machista* culture, a powerful misogyny in government, in the laws, and so on.

FIONA: I suppose for these reasons, the PRI's seven-decade rule was often referred to as "the Perfect Dictatorship." How did that patriarchal form of organization allow the party to keep such a strong grip on power for so long?

LYDIA: Last year, in the state of Oaxaca, a woman tried to become a politician. She wanted to run for mayor in her own little municipality, and the men tried to kill her for it. It is just an example of what happens all the time; it's not news for us. It's the same patriarchal system that works around the world. I don't have the answer, but I keep studying what is happening in Spain with the femicides. The psychotherapist Luis Bonino calls it "micro-machismo." Men wouldn't go out in the streets and be such machos without people judging them, but they're developing new ways to be macho. It is about control and submission and the superimposition of power onto women. It has to do with intense sexism, everywhere.

Learning from the Spanish, Mexico developed laws that are extremely sexist and patriarchal. For example, I saw a trial document from 1862 about the case of an Indigenous woman who was raped and then petitioned the police. At the trial, the judge allowed the lawyer and the district attorney, who was supposed to defend the woman, to start giving legal arguments to explain if the case could be taken by the judge. Both lawyers' speeches are amazing, because they outline exactly how a woman has no right over her body. And they do it based on legal facts. They are using the law and the Constitution to express the manner in which a woman is not the owner of her own body. The woman is Indigenous, so according to the law she does not possess enough intelligence to know if she provoked her attacker or not. In the end, the judge dismissed the case, saying that such an unimportant person should not take up the court's time, and the reason was that the man who had raped her was Spanish. Since he had no Indian blood, he had a right to defend himself, but he wasn't there, so the case was dropped.

I have the transcript of one of the judges' comments in the Supreme Court case that I brought forward. He said, "Why is this woman taking so much of the Supreme Court's time, when so many people get tortured in this country every day? Why should we take the time for her case?"

FIONA: That's quite a statement coming from a judge! What is behind it?

LYDIA: I think the feminist movement has been able to touch many areas of society, but the real powers that be are untouched. They have used all this discourse of gender and women's rights and so on because it is politically expedient, but they have not been touched fundamentally by feminist ideas and practices.

Fears of the Powerful

FIONA: Do you think they're afraid of feminism, of feminists? This is a prevalent fear of the powerful everywhere, after all.

LYDIA: Oh, yes. I think they're afraid of the idea of being emasculated by women. The men I accused of running the pedophile ring have said that the narcos [drug mafias] paid me to write about them, but of course nobody believes them. So they started to say that I'm a witch, that I'm doing something to them. I guess in some sense I am. I think that they're afraid of many things. They are afraid not of me, Lydia Cacho, but of the image of me. The social image I've created, how people see me as a powerful woman who doesn't get angry, who does not yell at people, but who is not submissive—a woman who is assertive and knows how to defend her dignity. They have no idea how to deal with that, because in their minds such a woman doesn't exist. Women in general for them are objects.

In their minds, they cannot process the idea of a woman with power that is not a patriarchal power. They have to make up something that is magical, out of this world, or evil. Then they all get really angry with me because I shed light on issues of violence, power, and injustice. They don't like that kind of light. They like to be under the light they create.

FIONA: This makes me think about the witch hunts, the systematic killing of women that was carried out in Europe during the capitalist transition and that was exported to the Americas in conjunction with colonial expansionism. This history draws a connection between the killing of women and dispossession. But the story also connects with modern forms of power and control of women's sexuality, and freedom more generally. What are your thoughts on sexuality and the refusal of fear? What could this refusal have to do with the creation of a different female experience?

LYDIA: I think by now we all know that the witch hunts had a lot to do with the elimination of female power. For the church, getting rid of women was crucial. I guess it has a lot to do with how they wanted us to be mutilated, as they mutilated themselves with cultural violence. When I was in Senegal working on issues of HIV-AIDS and clitoral mutilation, I talked to women who were doing mutilations to the kids. I talked to the grandmothers who were holding the little girls down to have their clitorises cut. They knew that if they didn't play the game, they would be pariahs in their own communities and the girls would never find anyone, any man who respected them or loved them. The women were so afraid of being thrown out of the tribe that they would rather agree to the rules of patriarchy than resist. They knew that the rules were no good; they told me so. But they also told me that these were the only rules under which they could stay alive.

I also interviewed a wonderful doctor. She had had an ablation when she was little and she told me about her life after she was cut. I guess it reminds us that we have to be very careful of the sense of belonging that society gives us. Our sexuality is so entwined with the idea of sexuality that is created by those who have the power to write about it. And the ones who had the power to write about it were religious men, and they were writing from the perspective of their amputated selves. They take maternity and say, "Okay, she is able to have a kid, but the kid belongs to society, so the body belongs to society when she's pregnant." And they mutilate you for that. And if a woman wants to have her rights, if she wants to be outside, she has to be like a man. She has to take power in a patriarchal way. If she doesn't, she becomes a pariah. That's what they're doing to me right now. The whole system is doing that to me, but I'm not getting into that game.

FIONA: Can you explain a little more what you mean?

LYDIA: First they told me the justice system would listen to me. Even though I didn't believe it, I went for it, because I wanted to prove that the system we have does not listen to women. So I took my case against the pedophiles and their powerful protectors all the way to the Supreme Court, and I was the first Mexican woman to sue a governor or an organized crime boss. I took the case to the highest levels because I wanted to show them that the system doesn't work. It doesn't work for a woman in general; it doesn't work for a woman who is defending the rights of girls to have happy lives free of violence, especially sexual violence. And if you analyze my case, you see that the more they tried to beat me, the more I just moved away— I was never submissive. I kept going and I was not a professional victim, as they wanted me to be. I do cry a lot, but I never cried on TV, never. So I wasn't what they expected: a crying woman, a victim, destroyed by the system. I'm not. If I'm going to cry I'll cry with the people I love. Here, I am a citizen, I'm a feminist, and I'm saying what I have to say.

Every time they tried to destroy me in the social ways that a patriarchal system tries to control women, they failed. The Supreme Court denied me justice. But the way they did it shows us what they are not willing to talk about. The Supreme Court decided not to talk about child pornography, and they decided that the issue was not the rape of the girls. They took the crime away from the centre of the discussion, the reason I took my case to the Supreme Court. They voted six against four to drop the case. If it had continued, they would have had to talk about the real issue, which was the rape of girls: the appropriation of the bodies of girls to be sold, used as things, to make money.

To do this, they took the case apart. They took away the issues regarding sexual abuse—even in the case of my arrest, my torture, they took all the sexual issues away—and they only discussed freedom of expression and whether the perpetrators violated my constitutional rights. But as they mutilated the case of its core issues, they didn't really have a case. So when it came to the last day, the pressure from society on the court was so intense that we thought we were going to win. It was amazing. It was something society took on for itself. It wasn't, "Lydia is going to win," it was, "Society is going to win." Even the media was saying that we were winning! The two female judges, who actually got there because of feminism, said that it was really bad what happened to the girls, and so on, but then voted against us. I think the lesson here is that the two women played the game to disassociate the issue of sexual violence from this case in order to stay in power.

This was such a powerful, high-profile case in two respects: one, it had to do with the sexual abuse of children, something that, obviously, really moves people. If it had been an adult pornography case, maybe nobody would have paid attention. This involved children, and people are really afraid of that. Not only that: so many people have been sexually abused as children. We don't even know how many. For whatever complex reasons, society took this case as its own case. It moved their souls and dislodged their traumatic memories.

There's another aspect to this, which has a lot to do with the way I was raised. My mom talked about sexuality all the time. I knew since I was a little girl that my body was my own and I would decide on my sex life and my erotic life. I didn't grow up with taboos. So the way I talked about this in my book and the way I investigated the case was in such a way that I didn't have any fear of going through that.

FIONA: Do you mean fear about your sexuality?

LYDIA: No. I guess when we write about sexual violence, I think we tend to express our own taboos. It's very hard not to do this. I think I'm lucky not to have internalized taboos regarding my sexuality. Because of this, I could ask the girls, the survivors of the abuse, things that nobody else would dare to ask. And at the same time, it liberated these girls from their own taboos. They were really young, and really didn't understand what had happened to them.

I started to understand that a young child reads sexual abuse and sexual violence completely differently from how an adult does. Adults impose their own taboos and ideas on child victims of sexual assault. A lot of the mothers of the abused kids told me their own stories of abuse. One told me her kid had been used for pornography since she was five years old, and when we got her out of there she was nine. The mother was a singer in a bar and had a troubled life. When we interviewed her, after a while she told us about how she had been raped by her father when she was little. She told her mother, and her mother sent her to live at her grandfather's house in Yucatan, and there her grandfather raped her and her uncle raped her. By fifteen she had left the house and was working in bars. She never decided to be a prostitute, but she said she would sometimes get paid for sex. And one day she was so sick of the trials and the media that she said, "Oh, listen to me, Lydia, she's already been used, so let's leave it at that! Let it go, that's life." I said, "Okay, do you really think that?" And we kept talking, and I said, "What would you do if, when you were abused by your father, your mother had recognized and acknowledged your pain and your fear and your anger, and she had left your father and gone with you to another place? Do you think your life would be different?" And then of course she cried and all, but it was an interesting development because she went on with the trial but decided not to talk to her daughter anymore about this issue, because she didn't know how to do it. Her personal view of sex is that it's something evil that we have inside that is to be used by men.

FIONA: Something women possess that others with more power want?

LYDIA: Exactly. And we have to learn how to give it to them. I learned so much, because even the youngest victims were really angry about what the pedophiles had done to them. It wasn't so much the act itself as the betrayal. They acted like nice men. They were sweet to the kids. They made them feel warm and loved. They gave them gifts and told them they were clever and sweet. And then half an hour later, they were raping them. So what truly, truly hurt them didn't exactly have to do with their sexuality. Because of their age, they didn't have a concept of it as we have. But this sense of betrayal, and the confusion caused by not knowing if giving these powerful men their bodies in exchange for their love was the right thing to do, was the source of great anguish. It had nothing to do with genital exchange; it was deeper than that. For the pedophiles, it was more about the appropriation of the body and the will of the children. And when you understand the psychology of it, it raises a lot of questions about how we deal with sexual violence and fear.

I believe most specialized psychology approaches it from a Freudian point of view. They don't have a concept of the different ways girls and boys deal with it. The children are not traumatized by the sexual act itself, but by the betrayal, by the appropriation of their body and soul. All these victims feared their captors. Their nightmares were not of these men raping them, but of them coming back to kill them. They didn't have nightmares of sexual abuse. They had nightmares of betrayal. So working with them through these issues of fear, I was working with my own fears. We're just beginning to understand what sexual violence means, in many ways.

7

SANDRA MORAN

Feminist Indignation

LMOST two decades after the 1996 signing of Guatemala's peace accords—an event that marked the formal end to a devastating civil war waged over four decades—another, undeclared, war on women rages on. According to official reports, between 2000 and 2012, over seven thousand women and girls were murdered in Guatemala. The office of Guatemala's Human Rights Procurator reports that up to 70 per cent of the murders have not been investigated, and in 97 per cent of cases, no arrests have been made. This violence echoes some of the most brutal aspects of the civil war, in which over two hundred thousand people, mostly civilian Indigenous *campesinos* (peasants), were killed, the overwhelming majority by the state's military and paramilitary forces. The Guatemalan women's movement played a central part in the peace process to end the war, and, thanks to the movement's tenacity, women have made some important social advances since 1996. But patterns of violence established during the war continue, and its aftermath has meant an official peace without justice, ravaged by widespread social violence. Putting a stop to the violence is severely hindered by Guatemala's stifling post-war climate of impunity, which women's movement activists argue is one of the war's most enduring legacies.

The issue has been receiving national and international attention thanks to the hard and dangerous agitation of the feminist movement, along with human rights advocates and the families and friends of victims. Drawing on the language used by the women's movement in Ciudad Juarez—a city on the US-Mexico border that has experienced a similar pattern of gender violence and impunity—Guatemala's women's movement asserts that the surge in murders and disappearances of women and girls amounts to a femicide. The charge of femicide, a juridical term for gendered genocide, is a way of politicizing the murders in the face of official victim-blaming and making the crime both public and globally resonant. One of the most vital grassroots women's groups organizing around the femicide in Guatemala is the autonomous feminist platform organization Alianza Politica Sector de Mujeres (Political Alliance of the Women's Sector). This coalition of women's groups, drawn from a range of social sectors, has been very publicly agitating for genuine social security that applies to everyone, which, by extension, means a halt to the impunity that continues to thwart Guatemala's post-war justice system.

Because of this work, the Sector's offices have been attacked, and its members routinely threatened. The break-ins have acted as both threat and message, clarified, in the case of a series of attacks that took place in June 2006, by the perpetrators' making off with only a mobile phone and the organization's fax machine, and their search of files containing critical information on the Sector's activities. To be sure that the message was unambiguous, the assailants poured blood on the floor around the office. In the week's second attack, they placed a shard of bloodied glass in the centre of the desk of a high-profile feminist activist, and one of the Sector's most public faces, Sandra Moran. To Sector activists, it is clear that these attacks are in retaliation for their increasingly visible and vocal role in the movement against the femicide and the impunity that fuels it. Contrary to the attacks' intended effects, the coalition of women's groups responded with a large and loud street demonstration in Guatemala City that brought several hundred women, men, and children out into the city's increasingly fearful streets. The demonstration of bold, public defiance featured music, poetry, a ceremony to honour the dead, a number of spirited speeches, and an impressive dose of political courage. "The attacks were a clear signal to tell us to be quiet and retreat," explains

Moran, "so we had to return very publicly to the street, to politics."

In this interview, Moran, who is also a musician and poet, talks about this work, and how feminists have resisted this pervasive climate of fear and impunity. A student activist during the height of the military dictatorship, Moran fled Guatemala in 1980 and lived in exile in Mexico, Nicaragua, and Canada. In 1996, she returned permanently to Guatemala to work with the women's movement and towards the realization of the peace process. In the interview, Moran shares her thoughts on Guatemala's contemporary women's movement, its analysis of power and autonomy, and the relationship between terror, impunity, and social control. She discusses the central role of the women's liberation movement in meaningful social change and points to some of the ways we can draw inspiration and direction from movements that are resisting fear in a world of dangerous places.*

FIONA: Can you provide some background on the Women's Sector and about the role of the women's movement in Guatemala's peace process?

SANDRA: The organization called the Women's Sector was formed in 1994. It was comprised of women's groups participating in the popular movement and emerged out of the need to make women's struggles and our presence within the popular movement more visible. It brought together thirty-one different women's organizations from across the political and social spectrum. We didn't know each other and had to work through issues of trust. From 1994 to 1996 we worked on expanding women's participation in the peace accords, and we achieved this participation, especially that of women in the capital, Guatemala City. But, since the participation of the whole country in the peace process was necessary, in 1997 we decided to form the National Women's Forum. By 1998 we were elaborating on a social movement of women, asking, "What do we, as women, want?" By 2000 we were focusing on public policy for women. From 1994 to 1998 much of women's organizing focused on the peace accords, and in 2000,

---

* An earlier version of this piece appeared in *WSQ* 37, nos. 3 and 4 (2007).

with the establishment of the Women's Secretariat, a distinct political structure was established within the state.

The peace process opened up a space for oppositional struggle, the struggle of women and other social movements. Both during and after the war, people were afraid of social organizations. They needed to feel they would be safe from repression. But after the accords, a problem arose in that there was an absence of a separate space for politics outside of the state. The government opened a space for social movements and then tried to control that space. Government officials were going abroad, to Europe, North America, and so on, and saying, "Look! The women are participating!" We tried to work with government because that was an important space at the time, yet once again, women were made invisible. We spent three years trying to open up that space, and finally we decided that we weren't going to do the state's work for it anymore.

FIONA: How did the Women's Sector reorient its program and activities at that point?

SANDRA: We began to try to open up a space for social movements. We started a school to encourage both women's political participation and their formation as political subjects. This is one of our major projects now, and we are participating in spreading these schools for women around the country. We are committed to organizing across difference and to figuring out how to valorize each other's work. The participants include local leaders, members of local organizations, and individual women. Some women are very poor, some middle class; some are Indigenous, others *mestizo* [a term used across Latin America to describe people of mixed Indigenous and European heritage]; some are literate and some illiterate. The facilitators come from the local areas. This grounding in the community is very important. So is an orientation towards self-reflection, which is a major part of what we do. We analyze the deep roots of violence, poverty, and inequality. We always ask ourselves, "Are we maintaining or changing the system? What am I doing in my everyday life to challenge the status quo?" We discuss racism, homophobia, classism, sexism, and our relationship to these powerful social forces. Of course, the theme of diversity—ideological, sexual, religious, ethnic, and sectoral (for example, rural, urban, peasant, teacher, student, and so on)—is key here.

The school is one concrete example of our efforts to politicize the women's movement and resist its co-optation. We are using a language of women's liberation rather than the vague and bureaucratic language of "gender" favoured by the official culture. The problem with the "gender perspective" is that it depoliticizes the movement. And we need to politicize it! In Guatemala there are tons of women experts in gender, but not in politics. After the UN conference on women in Beijing in 1995, the "gender" perspective took hold and the women's movement lost some of its political vitality. In our classes, for instance, we are not doing workshops on "empowerment" because we see this as an effect of the school, rather than something that is taught. I can't empower you and you can't empower me, but we can create a space to valorize our work, and, through working together and thinking about social change, we discover more about who we are as social and political subjects.

Power Over, Power To

FIONA: A debate that has been very important in the alter-*mundista* (or alter-globalization) movement, and is especially so in many Latin American autonomous movements in which women are especially active—for example, the Zapatistas in Mexico, the Movimento dos Trabalhadores Rurais Sem Terra (Landless Rural Workers' Movement) in Brazil, and the *piqueteros* in Argentina—is the question of political power: to try to take it, or to work to create it. In his 2002 book *Change the World without Taking Power*, John Holloway refers to this division in terms of an attitude of "power over" versus struggles for "power to." It is, it seems, also a crucial debate for feminists at this historical juncture. How is the Women's Sector engaging with this question of political power?

SANDRA: We are discussing what kind of power we're looking for: the power that dominates, or the power that supports us. We're looking for the power to be ourselves: to create power. "Power over" is not the only way to organize. How we relate to power is the key. In our work, for instance, we don't use the prevailing "empowerment" language. We are talking about how to potentialize—to facilitate the capacity to make decisions for the self, the community, the family, and so on. We are valorizing and discovering who we are, our values, and how our power is not about "tolerating" each other, but about respect and dignity. This is a politics of possibility within diversity—among women, among women and men, between rural and urban dwellers, and so on.

We are addressing the question of power between women and trying to open spaces for mutual support. The theme of power between women is very important in our work, and this is the basis of our focus on working towards genuine diversity in our movements. We are concerned with how we work concretely to overcome conflicts so that we can avoid the endless splits and breaks in the movement. At the same time, of course, we are not denying conflict or necessarily seeing it as always a problem. Rather, we are trying to work through conflict and harness it as a creative force in order to strengthen and nurture the movement. This is a question we're dealing with: how to sustain organizations and strengthen them. This is not just an issue of resources, but also of building relationships. We are not just about what we are going to do for other people. We are also reflecting on what we are doing for ourselves, and that process is yet to come. We have ideas, but no process to pursue them yet.

FIONA: In relation to the complex issues around power and representation, you mentioned the importance of visibility for the women's movement. Can you elaborate on what this means in terms of feminist organizing?

SANDRA: The question of visibility is vital. Again, we relate its significance to the question of diversity, which is central to our political project. A commitment to diversity is part of our ongoing political action. Two sectors have been most visible in the period following the peace process: women and Indigenous communities. For me, the most strategic union in Guatemala right now is between the Indigenous and women's movements. And this relates directly to the question of power. While the trade unions and peasant organizations generally focus primarily on economic concerns, the women's and Indigenous movements are talking about questions of power relations as well as economic questions. And, of course, both movements are really looking at how we relate to power. As women and Indigenous people, we are the majority of Guatemala's population.

Indignation

FIONA: The Women's Sector has been really impressive in using various techniques to highlight the visibility of the struggles of women and Indigenous people, and in addition to your murals, art, street performances, and pamphlets, you have a number of really interesting slogans. One of them, "Reclaiming Our Indignation and Demanding Justice," is particularly interesting in the way it invokes an ethos of revolutionary dignity. Indignation is an interesting term here that suggests both anger and justice. Is this call for indignation an appeal for focused, deliberate, and productive anger? Is it an antidote to political fatigue? Is there a connection between this slogan and what you discussed earlier about the question of harnessing conflict in a way that is movement building and useful, rather than divisive and destructive?

SANDRA: Indignation means that our anger is for something; it is moving towards something. But it is not just about reclaiming our anger; it is something more profound that touches the core. To recuperate indignation, as it is rooted in the act of asserting our dignity, is something that touches our human core. It refers to something we already had, but have forgotten over the years and through the fears. Perhaps we have forgotten because of the passage of time, or because of the fear that comes with remembering. From there, we express indignation in solidarity with others as human beings, not just because of our political alliances.

You recuperate and then you demand. And in Guatemala, demanding justice goes against impunity. So when we say justice, we're also fighting the impunity, which is so strong in Guatemala right now. The situation of insecurity is extreme. After the war, we have a very weak justice system. Now the justice system works for the wealthy and powerful. For the common person, it just does not function. For instance, the rich landowners have access to the law to maintain control of the land: who has access, how workers are treated, and so on. But if a woman wants to lodge a complaint because of violence in the home, the system doesn't work for her. The justice system is not there for her. This is how impunity works: some have access to justice and others do not. We need a justice system that applies to everybody. We are demanding a justice system based on democratic ideas, where the law is the same for everybody. What we have now is an anti-democratic, corrupt system, where personal problems are resolved through money and violence. Now the practice is that people exact their own justice. It goes like this: if I cannot resolve a conflict with you, I pay someone to kill you. That's how conflicts are being resolved. Nobody is going to punish me or ask anything at all. I want to do it, and I do it.

We have a history of impunity spanning over five hundred years: first with the Spanish and the Catholic Church, which implemented laws to control the Indigenous communities. Later, there was historical impunity: from the US's involvement in the coup against Arbenz [the reformist president of Guatemala] in 1954 and the counter-insurgency campaigns, to the Guatemalan military, where nobody was prosecuted for the murders and assassinations during the war. There is historical impunity for those who are killing all those women in Guatemala today. Corruption is part of that historical impunity, which operates from the community to the state level. Corruption is in the head, too; it affects how we relate to one another. Without justice, we have complete chaos and insecurity. That's what we're living with now.

The source of the post-war insecurity in Guatemala now is the exercise of power by a few over the majority, according to their own interests. The interests of specific sectors—the drug mafia, powerful business, the military, and imperialists—control justice through impunity. But of course, they are not the majority of the people. Capitalist society kills possibility; in it, everything is for sale and colonized, and its current neoliberal expression means the further negation of justice and dignity. When you are negated, you die. A person who has spent his or her life struggling for justice draws their energy from the possibility of change. If that's taken away, you get frustrated and depressed; you don't have energy for living, and that's what neoliberal globalization, religious fundamental-ism, and the other powerful forces at work right now, in Guatemala and around the world, do. To reclaim our indignation is to open up the space of knowledge about possibility and to regain our energy for social justice and genuine change.

Legacy of War

FIONA: Much of the Women's Sector's energy and public agitation has focused on the thousands of women who have been taken by force and murdered over the last several years. Women's groups are calling the violence a "fem-icide" to relay the extent to which this violence is organized and genocidal. Can you discuss how the women's movement is explaining this surge in violence amid the official peace?

SANDRA: The problem doesn't have a single root, but the first of many expla-nations I would point to is that we are living with the terrible effects of the war. The war devalued life and destroyed the justice system. The logic driving this war-related violence is the patriarchal idea that a woman is someone's property. Violence against the enemy's woman was the pre-dominant logic of the war. This logic says: "It is my property and I can do whatever I want with it." A gangster punishes another gangster by going after his woman, his property: his mother, wife, girlfriend, or daughter. This was the military strategy used in the war. To take revenge, I kill the woman of the enemy.

It is also a political strategy to impose fear and terror. As women are gaining space, this fear operates as a weapon to make them pull back, to stop women's public actions and resistance and return them to the domes-tic, private world. In Guatemala there are men who were employed in the war as killers and torturers, and where are they now? Many work as private police or in the national police. Others continue on in the mili-tary. And for us, we connect the murdered and missing women today with those murdered and disappeared during the war. This connection extends to the form of torture that marked the bodies of murdered peasants during the war. Those signs routinely reappear on the bodies of murdered women today.

The pattern of the war continues today in the next generation as well. Many youth are children of the war. They witnessed mutilated bodies on the streets. The legacy of all this violence is that we are all fighting among ourselves as a society and there has been no process to heal as a society—as private individuals, maybe, but not as a societal project.

FIONA: One of your main efforts has been to make the femicide a public issue, and it has received some attention in the international media and among high-profile human rights groups. Amnesty International has published a couple of reports on the femicide in Guatemala over the last two years. However, there has been virtually no mainstream coverage in the North American media. How is it being covered in the Guatemalan media?

SANDRA: The murders of women have certainly had a lot of media coverage. While this attention is helpful in publicizing the femicide, unfortunately the dominant messages reproduce fear through their treatment of the women as numbers and the menacing tone of the reports. There has been some good reporting and genuine efforts to get to the root of the problem; however, it is very complex and difficult to connect the phenomenon of the violence with this extraordinarily complex history. So, much of the reporting focuses on relaying numbers: "Two more women killed, five women killed," and so on. As they're counting and counting, the message is, "You women have to be careful!" And how do you be careful? "You stay home, watch how you behave with others, and watch how you dress, and the men will take care of you." We're saying "No!" We are not going to resolve the problem this way. *They* have to resolve it. We are not going to be silent.

Resistance

FIONA: What are some of the concrete ways in which the women's movement is resisting this politically charged climate of fear?

SANDRA: Resisting fear involves both an individual decision and a collective approach. Two years ago we hosted a visit from Esther Chàvez, a feminist activist from Ciudad Juarez who has been a central figure in the anti-femicide movement in that city. She came to Guatemala to share strategies on stopping the femicide, the impunity that fuels it, and the fear that envelops the lives of the inhabitants of both cities. Juarez, of course, has been the site of a very similar pattern of femicide, whereby hundreds of women have been murdered and disappeared since 1993, and Esther has been very publicly active in the movement to stop the violence and demand the prosecution of those responsible. That night, somebody broke into our office. The only thing they took was our extremely modest security system: a machine that records the numbers of those who call us. Taking this machine was a clear message. Up until then, we were in the streets, very publicly demanding security from the state. We pulled back then. No more public events, no more speeches or media presence—especially for me, because I've been the spokesperson and public face of the Women's Sector. Nobody left the office alone, and we all got cellphones. But then I was feeling even more scared! Two weeks later I called a meeting and said that this wasn't the way to go. They wanted us to collapse so that we didn't push the issue in the street. They wanted us to be quiet, and we'd given it right to them. This isn't a strategy. So we decided that that was enough. We then returned to our previous strategy of talking publicly, doing interviews in the media, and shouting in the streets, because for me, the public arena was security.

Another important incident took place last year at the demonstrations against the CAFTA [Central America–US Free Trade Agreement], when we took over the streets with comrades from across the movement to protest the neoliberal pact. The demonstration was huge, and the police response was very intense. They sent us running all over the city. As we scattered, there were many arrests, and even an order to arrest all the leaders of the demonstrations. Despite the fear that afternoon—generated not only from the direct repression at that particular moment, but, of course, out of the terrifying memory of Guatemala's historical violence—we decided that we should take the streets again. We determined that we had to retake the city—that given all we'd been through over the years and the real gains made in the ten years since the peace accords, we absolutely couldn't allow the streets to reside in the hands of the military or the police. Two days later we went back to the streets and took the city back. In spite of whatever tactical and philosophical differences that existed among the wide range of groups participating in the demonstrations, we were unified in the necessary desire to retake the city and to not give the military or police any reason to arrest or relaunch the violence of the previous days. We did it! This is one example of the collective struggle against fear.

8

GUSTAVO ESTEVA

Political Courage and the
Strange Persistence of Hope

USTAVO ESTEVA is an activist, writer, agriculturalist, and self-
described de-professionalized intellectual. My conversation with
Esteva took place at the Universidad de la Tierra (University of the
Earth), an autonomous, grassroots educational institution he helped
found in Oaxaca, Mexico. The school emerged out of many years
of activism and collaboration dedicated to the reconstruction of the commons in the face of intense pressures of privatization in Mexico, especially
in predominantly Indigenous and rural southern regions. For many years,
Esteva has worked closely with many of Mexico's Indigenous communities
and movements, including the Zapatistas in Chiapas. He has written widely
on theories of revolution, the urban and rural commons, human rights, and
ecological thought. He has contributed influential and controversial critiques of international development, food politics, and emancipatory education. Our conversation weaves together Esteva's reflections on his politically
committed life and his thoughts about the impact of the Zapatista rebellion
on Mexican society and political culture.

Esteva also discusses the violence and repression that was unleashed in
response to the Oaxaca commune of 2006, when a teachers' strike turned into

8

a major grassroots urban uprising against Oaxaca's state government. The uprising was ignited when the authoritarian state governor ordered a violent attack on the encampment of striking public school teachers in Oaxaca City's busy, touristy central plaza. Support for the teachers caught like fire and many people joined the encampment, which soon turned into an urban commune. The Oaxaca commune transformed the city for seven months. The movement evicted the police, distributed food, ran the barricades, and appropriated strategic channels of the communication infrastructure. The actions in the city inspired a political uproar across much of the state, and communities removed government representatives from small villages and large municipalities alike to protest the corruption, violence, and injustice of the neoliberal state. The movement started as a labour strike and quickly turned into a demand for the removal of the state governor, Ulises Ruiz Ortiz, who represented a set of neoliberal policies that had greatly exacerbated the presence of fear and insecurity in the everyday lives of the vast majority of the people. Ulises Ruiz symbolized the privatization of land and public services, the violent repression of dissidents, and an accelerating process of enclosure of the commons. Throughout the seven months of its life, the commune was subjected to intense, violent repression. Against that perilous backdrop, Esteva reflects on the role of systemic fear and the possibilities and challenges of resistance.

Beginnings

FIONA: Could you tell me a little bit about yourself, the experiences that led you to your participation in various grassroots movements over the years, and what inspired your turn to extensive studies on radical democracy and pluralism?

GUSTAVO: It is a very long story! I've been at this for fifty years. Of course, my motivations have changed a lot over those years. In the sixties it was the time of Che Guevara, and we felt an obligation to start a revolution. That's exactly what some friends and I tried to do by creating a kind of guerrilla group. Anyways, since the sixties I have been involved with many different movements. After coming back to the land of my ancestors to live in a small Indigenous village in Oaxaca, one of the first things we organized was the Center for Cultures in Dialogue. This was in the early 1990s, and we had a conviction that perhaps the main issue of the twenty-first century would be interaction among cultures. And we wanted to explore the possibilities of a real dialogue. We started asking, "How can we interact with people from other cultures coming to Oaxaca from North America, Japan, Finland, and so on?" But our main emphasis was to have a space for dialogue among the cultures of Oaxaca. Accompanying Indigenous people in dialogue is not just talking. It's not even transcending; it is working together.

In the late 1990s, the Indigenous communities of Oaxaca adopted a very strong position against the education system. An Indigenous forum declared public schools to be the main tool of the state for the destruction of Indigenous cultures, and that the revolutionary teachers' union was an accomplice of the state in this destruction. Some communities started to close schools, to take initiatives beyond education and beyond the schools, reclaiming again the learning processes of their children. At one point some of these communities started to say, "Our children are learning better than they were in the school, but because they don't have any certification, what will happen if they want to learn more?" Out of these discussions we created Universidad de la Tierra in Oaxaca. It is basically a university for young Indigenous people. To study here, students don't need any certification of prior studies. They need to know how to read and write and have a clear idea of what they want to learn. Then we support the learning process. This is a community of learners. We have no established hierarchies, curriculum, or formal classes. The students learn by doing what they want to learn. If a student wants to become an agrarian lawyer, we send him or her to do an apprenticeship with an agrarian lawyer.

In addition to my collaborations with these educational organizations, I have been associated with the Zapatistas since they appeared in 1994, and they invited me to be an adviser in 1996 when they entered negotiations with the government. Since then I have been involved in many different activities, including the Other Campaign that started in 2006 and an international colloquium on Planet Earth and anti-systemic movements. Perhaps my motivation to participate in social movements is that I cannot be otherwise. It is a way of living. I cannot be separated from my society. I am in this society associated with the people who have, throughout history, been the most oppressed and exploited people: Indigenous people, peasants, and marginalized urban dwellers. One of the main motivations, which is very pertinent for our conversation, is hope. Hope is what nourishes my activities with social movements. I think that hope is the very essence of popular movements. People mobilize because they have hope, because they nourish the hope. Here in Mexico we have a very beautiful expression of hope: *abrigo esperanzas*. It doesn't mean that I have hopes, but that I protect, care for, and nourish hopes, because hope is neither expectation nor the conviction that something will happen. As Václav Havel once said, hope is basically the conviction that something makes sense, whatever may happen. My personal involvement with movements is based in this kind of hope. What does not make any sense is acceptance of, or resignation to, the current situation.

There is another element of my motivation. I abandoned my guerrilla attempt in 1965 due to a series of events that is perhaps not pertinent for our conversation. But the main and relevant reason was that I observed the violence that we were imposing on ourselves and that we therefore wanted to impose on the whole of society. At that point I became affiliated with non-violence. I did not abandon my ideas, or the kinds of struggle I was involved with, but I did abandon the idea of violence as a path to social change. And this stance was challenged during the first week of 1994, when the Zapatistas appeared on the scene. I found myself in a very serious moral conundrum. I asked myself, "Why are you so happy, so enthusiastic, about the Zapatistas if they are killing each other in Chiapas? Are you not for non-violence? Why do you like the idea of the Zapatista struggle so much?" At that point I started to reread Gandhi, and I discovered something that I had not read before and that is particularly relevant for this question of hope and fear. Gandhi's son asked his father, who had recently survived an assassination attempt, "What should I do if someone tries to kill you? Should I practice non-violence and observe how he hurts or kills you?" Gandhi's response was to smile and say, "What you must not be is a coward. If non-violence is a supreme virtue, cowardice is the worst of vices. You must not be a coward. The weak have no option but violence or passive resistance. It would be criminal on my part," he said, "to preach non-violence to a mouse that is about to be devoured by a cat. If I am preaching non-violence to the people in India, it is because I don't see why 300 million Indian people are afraid of 150,000 British people. It is because they are strong that they should use non-violence."

This was the perfect story for the case of the Zapatistas. They were clearly the weak side in the conflict. They had tried everything. We know that now. They struggled through political organizations, social organizations. They tried various kinds of mobilizations, such as that impressive march from the highlands, when three thousand people walked five hundred miles from Chiapas to Mexico City to present their claims. The people were dying like flies—of hunger, curable disease, and the oppressive local structures of power. They did everything and nobody heard, not the government and not society. After trying everything else, they tried the uprising of 1994. I think it was their last resort. I am convinced that at that time they had no hope of a military victory.

But the uprising of civil society surprised them. Millions of people poured onto the streets all over the world in support of the Zapatistas, telling them, "You are not alone!" and "We are with you!" The Zapatistas, in turn, became strong. That is the context in which they became the champions of non-violence in Mexico, because of this position of civil society. And they have been very respectful, firing no weapons, ever, despite endless provocations by the state, militaries, and paramilitaries, since January 12, 1994. They have shown incredible restraint and capacity for non-violence, and great ingenuity in how to resist.

Global Fear

GUSTAVO: Yet fear is generated day after day in Chiapas. The fear is circulated through propaganda on the radio, and through the violent threats of the paramilitaries and the authorities. Day to day, for years, the Zapatista communities have heroically resisted these aggressions. The government and paramilitaries are always attempting to reoccupy the land, and we need to support the communities who live there, not only in principle but actively in Mexico and internationally, and tell them they are not alone. We need to be able to demonstrate to the government that by attacking the Zapatistas they are attacking all of us, millions of us, everywhere.

Fear, as the writer Eduardo Galeano has claimed, is now a global fear. It's a global fear not only because of the specific violence—the violence of the police or the violence of the narco-traffickers—but it is also a fear about everything. A global fear of hunger, or fear of food. You can be afraid of not having food, or you can be afraid of the kind of food you have.

Here in Oaxaca, fear is ever-present in the aftermath of the violence surrounding the social uprising against the state in 2006. We still don't have information about the numbers of disappeared. One woman told us, "They disappeared one of my sons. If I present this information in public they will disappear the other." We were collecting facts about the situation and wanted her denunciation, but we could understand very well her reaction. She was really intimidated. She couldn't put the life of her other son at risk. There are many people who don't want to talk about what happened here; they are escaping from reality, hiding in their houses. There is, on the one hand, a sense of helplessness and desire to escape, but there is also another reaction, which is one that I'm really afraid of. That is the reaction of rage and violence. I classify this reaction as part of the reaction to fear.

For example, during the uprising of 2006, there were many areas of Oaxaca in which the old *cacique* [local political boss] structure was finally broken, and people seized the possibility of kicking the entrenched political class out of government, occupying the plazas, and so on. Well, these local caciques are now trying to recover what they had. They are trying to come back to government. Some of the people who displaced them are saying, "We cannot allow these caciques to come back, because they will kill everyone they see as responsible for them losing power!" The next thing people say is that the only way to resist this is to prepare with weapons, because these men are armed and they will try to take us out of here with their weapons. This makes the possibility of violent confrontation all over Oaxaca very real.

What we have at this point is the explosion of expressions of civil war, not a popular uprising, in many parts of Mexico. The situation is rooted in massive discontent with neoliberal policies—with the general situation of increasing repression and the state's use of the police and the army as a substitute for politics. The system is falling apart.

Coalitions of the Discontented

FIONA: The Oaxaca uprising of 2006 was a high-profile example of the many pockets of resistance to neoliberalism across Mexico today. The state's repression of the teachers detonated an outpouring of discontent that quickly became a coordinated resistance to impunity, neoliberalism, and the political class all at once. The movement's quick, confident, and exuberant transformation of the city into a commune was surprising to many. Can you talk about what links the many initiatives going on across Mexico today?

GUSTAVO: We use the category of localization to express an alternative to both globalization and localism. For hundreds of years, communities have been entrenching themselves to resist colonialism, to resist development, to resist capitalism, to resist the innumerable forms of repression waged against them. Localism and localists sometimes become fundamentalists, but we are convinced that locality can, over time, resist the current tsunami of capital. What the people are doing, as far as we can see, is affirming themselves in their own places. They are not abandoning their places. But at the same time, they are opening their minds, their hearts, and their arms to create coalitions of the discontented, coalitions of opposition.

What the Zapatistas have been trying to do with the Other Campaign is connect these pockets of resistance to organize a peaceful, democratic uprising. The reason that we don't have that network yet, as far as I can see, is the political situation in Mexico. All the campaigns against the

Zapatistas, particularly from the left, have prevented the possibility of really creating an association among all these pockets of resistance. Our current situation could move in the opposite direction, towards a series of confrontations resulting, in some cases, in very vicious violence. It is not a revolutionary context. It is not a context for revolution with a clear direction, objectives, and so on.

From what I can see, people are reacting in two main ways to the state's active promotion of fear: with either intimidation or rage. I am very hopeful, only because I think that perhaps the majority will react with serenity and organization. That is what I find the most interesting and positive reaction that I can see. And I think the Indigenous communities are showing great leadership in elaborating forms of thoughtful organization in the face of enormous fear and violence on the part of the state and the paramilitaries.

In Oaxaca, Chiapas, and other parts of Mexico today, you can plainly see that Indigenous communities have centuries of experience with political repression. As a result, they know how to react. In response to the intense repression raining down on communities around Mexico today, I have heard some people in a number of Indigenous villages say, "We need to play *Tlakwatche*." A Tlakwatche is a strange animal, like a big rat, that has a weird reaction when a predator attacks. It pretends to die. When the predator leaves, the Tlakwatche gets up and leaves. To "play Tlakwatche" means to pretend the movement is over, to pretend everything is okay now as a way to stop the repression, to go deeper in the organization and prepare for the next phase of the struggle. This is one way of dealing with the escalation of political fear that I'm hearing about from the grassroots level of the villages. They are pretending that the movement is over while they prepare themselves for the next phase.

In the case of Oaxaca, because of the blindness of the political classes, our movement has been deepening and strengthening beautifully. During the popular uprising in 2006, people risked everything to remove the governor from office. But if we had been able to do it, the movement would have dissolved. Instead, the failure to remove him prompted people to seriously reflect on the nature of politics as it is—on electoral processes, formal democracy, and representative democracy. This has been an enormously important experience, which involves thousands, perhaps millions, of people in Oaxaca who have strengthened their awareness of the actual situation. Indeed, Oaxaca is a very good example of a change that appears to be happening all over the world: widespread disenchantment with formal representative democracy. Even in areas of the world where people can believe in the electoral process itself, because they have free elections and votes are respected, people are disenchanted with the outcome. Even if people from the left are elected, it is irrelevant. But instead of paralysis, people have responded to this situation with a very interesting movement to apply the experience of what we would call radical democracy, currently practiced in Indigenous villages, to the whole of society. The conflagration of 2006 was, in a very limited and peculiar sense, an experiment in these ideas and practices of radical democracy, only this time it was applied not to a village but to a city of six hundred thousand inhabitants.

Security without the Security State

FIONA: The fact that the police and military had been kicked out of the city and yet crime and violence hit a ten-year low is one of the most fascinating and instructive dimensions of the 2006 commune experiment. Can you talk about that aspect of the social uprising?

GUSTAVO: We had no police for four months, and we had none of the usual problems—not even traffic problems. The organization of the city's everyday functions was, for once, in the hands of the people. During those four months, according to human rights organizations, we had less violence, fewer crimes of every kind, fewer assaults, and fewer injuries than in any other comparable period of the last ten years. The city was clean, and it operated very well without the government. It was a kind of massive experiment, and the experience is now lodged in the collective memory.

In 1996 the Zapatistas invited us to reflect on what it is we can do at the local level to advance democracy and social justice without the political parties and without the government. After a few months of reflection, we had a joke that if there is something we can't do at the local level and we need someone in Mexico City to make that decision, then the job should be designated to Mexican ambassadors in other countries. To our surprise, we began to discover that we could do almost everything by ourselves, without the parties and without the government. At that time, this vital realization was still theoretical. It was a possibility, a process of reflection more than action. But ten years after the Zapatistas' proposal, this process of reflection did produce an effect. During the months of the Oaxaca uprising, we experienced different ways in which we could handle our lives without the political parties, the government, or official leaders, because our movement was a movement without such leaders. This experience and its ongoing resonance is my main source of hope today. My hope is that the majority of people will react with this kind of peaceful, democratic struggle, which aims to extend radical democracy to the whole of society. My hope is that many people will have the sanity and the courage to react this way to fear.

FIONA: Given the typical fear of chaos and "ungovernability" associated with political upheaval, this seems to be a very important feature of the story of the uprising. You have written about this experiment in the grassroots organization of a city, but it has received little attention outside of Mexico. Could you talk about how people's experience of safety transformed without the state during that period? Did that experience challenge the hegemonic idea that the state provides at least a framework for security?

GUSTAVO: In Mexico, particularly among the social majorities, we don't associate security with the state. Quite the opposite. After so many years of corruption and violence, we feel insecure when we see the police or the army. This is the general feeling, but the middle and upper classes clearly associate security with the state and feel insecure before the people. I think that during the uprising in 2006 it was very, very clear for most of us that the major source of insecurity was the police. They created their own incidents of violence in order to blame the movement, especially the Popular Assembly of the Peoples of Oaxaca [known by its Spanish acronym, APPO], for causing insecurity. They organized specific attacks—

kind of guerrilla attacks against the civilians, but also against other non-affiliated people—so they could blame APPO. It quickly became very clear that the only real security, which includes both the feeling of security and actual security, depends on the social fabric. It requires organization. Having a strong social fabric does not only mean that you know the people around you. It also requires that you have the organization and you have the autonomy to create mutual protection. This was an experience we had during the months of the 2006 social uprising.

FIONA: In addition to the deluge of harrowing images of violent state repression, images of people celebrating, having fun, and socializing also poured out through the global alter-media network. What role did fiestas, friendship, parties, and social life in general play in creating the temporary space of freedom and security that you and others have written about?

GUSTAVO: The fiesta is one of the most important expressions of community in Oaxaca. The fiesta is the manner in which a whole community comes together without hierarchies. When people take on the organization of the fiesta, they provide a vital service to the whole community. Annual celebrations have a very important role in a community's social fabric, for they open up an opportunity to cure some community conflicts and interpersonal wounds that may have erupted over the previous year. During the fiesta, people who have stopped talking with each other, for whatever reason, can come together and reclaim their friendship. This tradition is very strong in Oaxaca. And it has helped to keep the social fabric going for centuries.

This tradition is generally associated with community life in the countryside, but what we did not know prior to the uprising in 2006 is how important these traditions are in the big cities, too. We did not know that there was something like a popular movement in the *colonias* [shantytown settlements], and that this social fabric is very strong. We didn't know how much people relied on their community ties and how they nourished those connections during the movement. There was a section on Radio Plantón that was called Amor de Barricada [Love at the Barricades], featuring stories of love blossoming at the barricades during the nights of fear as people prepared themselves for the attacks of the police. It was friendship, love, and this social fabric that created the real strength of the movement.

FIONA: How do you think systemic violence and fear affect this social fabric?

GUSTAVO: In telling these stories, we need to remember that in addition to the violence of the government and its paramilitaries, we also had violence on the side of the movement. We had young people who had been humiliated, attacked, and ostracized by society. And when the movement erupted, these people were really full of rage. At the beginning, their participation felt like an expression of revenge. Young people of the *barrios* [popular neighbourhoods] have been attacked by the police, in many different ways, for years. They have no experiences of the police and the government other than humiliation, oppression, and discrimination. So when the revolt began, the reaction among some people who had been subjected to this constant humiliation took the form of a kind of revenge. It was not political conviction. It was an opportunity to adopt another position. In time, they began to enter the discussion at the barricades and to gain a kind of political awareness. But still they had rage in their hearts.

This was very clear at an acute moment in the conflict, during the government's attack on the university. At that point, thousands of people came to the university full of rage. The movement's goal was to protect University City. It was a symbolic defence of the university. But there were ten to fifteen thousand people, some coming with slingshots, Molotovs, and so on, wanting to attack the police. I saw one banner during the march to Mexico City that read "*Pinche gobierno ya ni su guerra nos cumple* [Stupid government, you don't even fulfill your war]." This meant they had been waiting for the police to attack so they could react. They were training with stones and slingshots, preparing for a war with the police. And the police did not come. This was an expression of this rage that was also in the movement.

It really isn't productive to present just a romantic story about the movement, to say everything was perfect and we were doing everything well. Yes, there was a lot of rage on the people's side of this struggle, and some people reacted with this rage. Of course, this was used by the provocateurs. The movement was infiltrated constantly, and there was no way to prevent it. And then this rage was used to provoke a confrontation with the police, and then to justify the repression. This is inevitable with this kind of movement. This is something that requires more reflection, more work, and more organization. One of the things we are doing is holding workshops for reflections on non-violence. We need to make space for reflection on how we can keep struggling peacefully and democratically with non-violence, and how one can process this rage, to transform it into courage—political courage of the movement. That is not easy with this kind of government and the kind of political class we are dealing with; they are nourishing this rage every day, with impunity, with aggression.

Political Courage

FIONA: How would you define political courage?

GUSTAVO: I think you need a lot of courage to confront both the dominant ideas and the dominant practices. Courage becomes political when the expression of this courage is dedicated to recovering an older meaning of politics as the common good. When you're trying to organize to create a common good, it is not just to express your personal rage because of the very real offences you have suffered. It is to transform that rage into collective courage for the common good. Building the common good, as we can see very clearly in many parts of the world today, means going beyond capitalism.

The widespread disenchantment with representative democracy is also disenchantment with capitalism. I think more people are coming to the conclusion that we have had enough—that this specific system will not bring about any kind of good for any of us. We are increasingly aware that capital has a more voracious appetite than ever, but it doesn't have the stomach to digest all the people it wants to control. More and more people are made dispensable, the leftovers capital cannot use. The Zapatista expression "*Ya Basta* [Enough]!" captures well people's response to the injustice of the current situation, no matter what label it is given.

If you ask people on the street, people in the villages, "Are you anti-capitalist?" they will look at you perplexed. But if you listen to them, you find they are against this present system of exploitation and domination, and they are trying different initiatives to challenge it. In this way, they are expressing political courage in the interest of creating the common good. In Oaxaca this is inescapable. The practice of *tecio* [village-based communal labour] that you find in rural communities is an experience of the common good. People know that political activities are part of the common good, and they have a very clear definition of the common good. In that sense, people have an experience here in which every "I" is a "we." At the village level, people don't belong to a community; they are the community. Because of this relationship, political courage is embedded in the definition of their being. When they are trying to defend their community, that is an act of political courage. That is something embedded in your heart, as a definition of your own self. You are not separate from that interest. You don't have your own self-interest on one side and then the interest of the community on the other. Your personal interest is the interest of the community. We are using this worldview as an inspiration to nourish that kind of feeling in other people who do not feel this way because they have been constructed as individuals: people in the city, in the middle classes, or even in the popular *barrios* who are no longer part of a community in the traditional sense. And now many of these people are expressing this kind of political courage.

FIONA: Do you see this idea of political courage as a means to social and individual disalienation?

GUSTAVO: The barricades set up around the city to keep the police, military, and paramilitaries out during the 2006 revolt provided a magnificent place to nourish this kind of political courage. They were clearly an expression of personal, heroic sacrifice for the common good. People who spent their days and nights at the barricades were not gaining any personal, individual benefit for staying there every night for months. But it was a kind of commitment to the common good that was itself transformative. The barricades provided an opportunity for young people to talk with older people. In regular life, they don't talk. The barricades provided the perfect situation in which to talk. They provided a space where the energy and vitality of young people mixed with the wisdom and experience of the old people. It was a very important, interesting point of contact.

Temporalities of Hope and Fear

FIONA: Hope is a future-oriented concept; it signals a temporality of waiting and patience. This temporality of hope has often harnessed a politics of fear—fear that something worse will happen if the emancipatory desires of some are not sacrificed to this idea of the future. Given this backdrop, how do you think the concept of political courage connects to a politics of hope?

GUSTAVO: We are not thinking of a means to an end. We are not thinking of seizing political power and then commanding people's lives. We are trying to express what it is we can do today to transform society today. We are trying to represent the change we want in terms of the transformations that can be implemented every day. I think there is an increasing awareness that capital is basically a social relation, and we have been suffering under this kind of social relation. Building on this, we are trying to create a different kind of social relation in order to not be trapped in the social fabric of capital. For example, when you are a worker in a company and you create an organization like a union, you are working for capital. You are, in a sense, operating under conditions imposed by capital. You are trapped in the logic of capital. Even if you have a very independent union, you are struggling for your own interests with capital. You are not playing your own tune. You are playing the tune of capital.

We are trying to generate other kinds of social relations. We know all the limitations. We have been drawing inspiration from Paul Goodman's definition of daily life, which poses this challenge: suppose your side of the revolution won. Now think what you would be doing in that perfect society. You are no longer struggling against capital. You are already in the society of your dreams; what is it that you want to do? Do that today, said Goodman. Once you grapple with this idea, you find it isn't so easy to define the perfect society. Of course you will find obstacles, and you will need to remove them, go around them, go above them. But then your politics will be concrete and practical. You will not be dancing to the tune of the oppressor. You will be trying to find your own way. This is what we are trying to do here. We are trying to transform our today in the image of tomorrow. It is not trying to have an idea of tomorrow as something in the future, or what will happen once we are in power, but something that we can create today.

FIONA: Can you talk about some concrete practices that attempt to manifest this sense of a revolution in everyday life?

GUSTAVO: Let's go back to the barricades. The organization of the barricades was very important in this respect, because it fostered an experience of gratuity, of non-economic relations. The experience of social life that people had on the barricades occurred against a backdrop of severe economic crisis, so this element of non-economic exchange proved to be very important.

Oaxaca is an economic disaster. Small producers in Oaxaca are in agony because they can no longer sell what they're producing. This was happening before the uprising. For example, there was a women's cooperative in the village of Etla that had forty cows. They made the best butter in the world. Now they are trying to sell their cows because they can't sell the butter. Today the butter we find in the markets is from New Zealand.

To counter this, we are using local currencies for the direct exchange of what we produce. We are talking about *prosumidores*, meaning producers and consumers together. We are both. We develop relations of direct exchange between producers. There is everyday bartering in the markets, but you cannot live on that kind of bartering alone. Now we are creating a local currency to facilitate exchange. And you can see in that local currency what kind of social relations are established. People are bringing their eggs, lettuces, and so on to trade. Recently, I saw a woman giving a guy a massage in exchange for three kilos of chayotes. It was an exchange of goods and services. This is the kind of thing we need, and these are the types of things that are generating new kinds of social relations.

I can give many different examples like this, where people are creating these pockets, and in so doing they are trying to escape the logic of capital. These are very concrete images of the new, anti-capitalist society that we want to create. We are not waiting for a kind of utopian dream. We are trying to generate these ways of being in our daily lives today, while knowing all the limitations of these initiatives. The Zapatista communities are exposed to every kind of pressure, from the military, the paramilitaries, and the government, but they have created a way of living, a way of governing in and against a capitalist society. We are not living on Mars; we are living on this planet, recognizing all our limits and the problems that we face in the real world. This is one of the main sources of hope. More and more, people are very discontented with the current system, with capitalism, and with the political regime of formal democracy. It is easy to fall into desperation. But people see that making another world is possible—not in the future, but today.

At the end of an international gathering, the Zapatistas said that we are not here to change the world. This is something that is very difficult, and perhaps even impossible. Their aspiration, they said, is to create a whole new world. There was great applause. Yes, to change the world is next to impossible. But to create a whole new world is a pragmatic goal. To bring this point closer to where we are at this moment, we have created this space here in the Universidad de la Tierra. To change the educational system in Mexico is next to impossible. You cannot change one million teachers and the Ministry of Education. But you can create an alternative to the system. You can create an alternative system for learning. And so, instead of fighting against the dominant educational system, we are creating a real alternative, and then it can be applied to everything.

In a sense, I think that this is the most effective tool to fight against capitalism. The struggle against capitalism is not to denounce corporate power. Of course we want to do that, but it is not the most important element of the anti-capitalist struggle. The most important dimension is our efforts to change the kind of domination that we have in our hearts and minds—the kind of surrendering to capitalism associated with the possibility of creating another world.

FIONA: What do you think we can learn from resistant practices in places and moments of danger like you have been experiencing in Oaxaca before, during, and in the aftermath of the uprising?

GUSTAVO: The main lesson is the old lesson about balance. More and more, the political classes have infiltrated the various movements to create provocations and thereby give a kind of legitimacy to their violence. During the revolt of 2006, there was a moment in which we couldn't control the violence on our side, and in that moment, we created an opening for the repression. More and more, the government is deploying the force of the police and the military when its hold on power is shaken. But it needs pretexts to do this, and the problem is that our own violence, our own rage, can give them the pretext they need. During the uprising, every time we used non-violent tactics, we succeeded. When, for example, we hosted a grassroots, oppositional Guelaguetza festival against the fake, consumerist version promoted from above, there was a real danger of confrontation with the police. Some young people were confronting the police, and every time they confronted them, the police advanced two blocks. There was a moment when the police were four blocks from a huge concentration of people. There was real danger. A group of people suggested that instead of fighting with the police, we should sit on the floor. At this point we had a thousand people sitting on the pavement, and the police didn't know what to do with that. They knew very well how to fight. They had the shields and so on. After half an hour they left. That initiative protected the fiesta, the success of democratization. That's just one example of what we need to learn, and that with violence we will not.

This is not a pacifist statement. I started this interview talking about the possibility that the Zapatistas would use their weapons to protect their land. It is not that they want to do it, but they can be forced by the impossible circumstances. And they have the organization; they are very aware of the risks they are taking. It is our experience in these situations of extreme violence that non-violence has been very successful. But to use non-violence, you need to be strong. If you are weak, you have no option.

When you can define the politics of "one no and many yeses," you accept the plurality of the world while affirming our shared rejection of this system. But we accept that we have different views and ways of life, and are advancing in different directions. If we recognize the differences, then I think we can be really strong. This is how you become the struggle.

9

WENDY MENDEZ

Remembering the Disappeared, Revealing Hidden Histories of Resistance

W ENDY MENDEZ is a Guatemalan theatre artist, educator, and political activist. In the late 1990s, Mendez cofounded the Guatemalan section of HIJOS, an acronym (which spells "children" in Spanish) for Sons and Daughters for Identity and Justice against Oblivion and Silence. The group is part of a pan-continental movement formed by the children of leftist political activists who were disappeared by the military dictatorships of Latin America's "dirty war" period. Guatemalans endured one of the twentieth century's most protracted wars. During four decades of conflict, hundreds of thousands of people were killed, disappeared, or sent into exile. And although the war came to an official end with the signing of the peace accords in 1996, the violence and political persecution that ravaged Guatemalan society continues to this day. Such intense violence and loss leaves no one unscathed, and a palpable sense of danger, fear, and anguish runs through the sinews of everyday life. As people grapple with the fallout of decades of militarization, Mendez, along with many of the conflict's survivors, agitate for what she calls the necessary "de-militarization of the mind."

Mendez's mother was disappeared by the Guatemalan military during the height of the repression in the early 1980s. After many years of exile in

Canada, Mendez returned to Guatemala in 1999, where, along with the children of other dissidents who vanished during the war, she founded HIJOS. Operating within an atmosphere of ongoing tension, stark fear, and lingering sadness, the group uses murals, graffiti, and other forms of street art, along with public theatre and political protest, to open spaces for discussion and debate about the atrocities committed during the time of military rule. As Mendez explains, HIJOS activists see the restoration of a collective memory of resistance (a memory that the military has dedicated itself to destroying through brutal repression) as essential to the contemporary struggle for justice and against impunity in Guatemala. A public reckoning with the history of fear, she argues, is a crucial step in "de-militarizing" Guatemalan society. Our conversation starts with Mendez's reflections on imprisonment, loss, exile, and return. It then turns to a discussion about HIJOS's extraordinary politico-artistic work and the philosophy driving the group's audacious street theatre, legendary graffiti, and provocative mural projects. HIJOS's work has been very important in Guatemala, explains Mendez in this interview, because they insist on rescuing historical memory, collective memory, and individual memory.*

Remembering

FIONA: Let's start with your background. How did you become involved with the collaborative political and artistic work that you do?

WENDY: I was born in Guatemala in 1974, during the war. My parents were active in the revolutionary movement, and growing up with them was a very beautiful experience. We were always participating in different political activities, and that was really fun. At home, we listened to the music of political artists like Inti-Illimani or Victor Jara—although very quietly, because at the time, the authorities did not think this music was

---

* This interview was conducted in the summer of 2009, prior to many critical events in the fast-moving and intensely contentious world of Guatemalan post-war politics. Our conversation, carried out over several days, represents both a snapshot and long view of a still-unfolding story.

proper—and our parents would try to motivate us to tell them what we heard in the songs, what the music meant to us.

I have a lot of memories of my mom. When we were walking on the street running an errand or something, she used to always point out the kids shining shoes in Guatemala City's central plaza. She would ask us, "Why do you think those children are working? They are your age— why are you not working? Why do you think people are living on the streets?" My brother and I would say something like, "Oh, maybe they lost their jobs." We were always encouraged to think about the reality of our surroundings, to understand why people were fighting for the right to education, the right to health, to land, and so on. We knew that in one way or another our parents were involved in the social movement, because there was a lot of activity going on around where they worked and at the university where they studied. We knew there was a war going on in Guatemala and that it had begun a really long time ago. One of my grandmothers remembered the US invasion in 1954, when they came with planes to overthrow [reformist president] Jacobo Arbenz Guzmán. She used to tell stories about how people were so scared because they had never seen those types of planes before.

We understood that there was risk in the work our parents were doing because a lot of people were being killed for political reasons. Anyone displaying opposition to the government was treated as an enemy of the government and considered a target for killing or disappearing. And on the eighth of March, 1984, that is exactly what happened to my mother. When my brother and I came home from school that day, we found that police and soldiers had raided our home, along with every second house in the neighbourhood. Normally by the time we arrived at home the other neighbourhood kids would be outside playing. But on that day, we immediately noticed that no kids were outside. All the windows and curtains were shut in the surrounding homes. There was just silence. When we went into our house we found about twelve soldiers and police officers. The whole place had been searched. It looked like a big struggle had taken place, with furniture upside down and so on. As soon as we walked in and began to take all this information in, the door shut behind us.

They sat us down and began to question us about the whereabouts of our parents. They asked all kinds of questions about where they worked, what time they came home, their names, the names of their friends, and we began to understand what was happening. The fear was present. We just said that we didn't know. For instance, when they asked, "What's your mother's name?" we would answer, "Mom." They began to get really angry with us because they knew that we were being very selective about what we were saying. We were there for many hours, and on different occasions they would threaten us in different ways to get us to talk. They would say to me, for example, "If you don't give the information that we want, we are going to kill your brother." Or they would turn it the other way around. We began to get really scared, because night was coming and they weren't leaving.

They took us outside in the backyard and stood us against a wall. One of the soldiers pointed his gun at us, playing and laughing. We were just so scared. We were crying and would say to them, "Please don't do this, leave us alone, go away." They just kept laughing. At one point, my brother was hurt because it seemed like they were going to shoot me, and he stepped in front and tried to push one of the soldiers away. The solider punched him in the head with his rifle butt. I went to help him and the soldiers were swearing and yelling, "Don't be bothering us!" It felt like they were going to execute us. And then my mom appeared.

We didn't realize that she had been inside the house all this time. We barely recognized her because she had been beaten so badly. But her voice was clear. And she started screaming at them, "Don't touch my children!" I remember that one of the guys pointing his gun at us suddenly turned around and shot her once. She collapsed, holding her stomach, and they just picked her up and took her inside the house.

We were then brought back inside the house and they forced my brother and I to eat bananas that had already been peeled. We were wondering what was going on—why were they were feeding us now? Of course, we didn't want to eat anything, especially anything that they gave to us. But they forced us, and immediately we began to feel really sleepy and weird. They sat us down and grabbed some pliers out of a box and began to peel off my mother's fingernails. We shut our eyes and screamed at them to stop, and they didn't. They would open our eyes forcibly so we would see. You could see that my mother was in pain, but she would just look at us to try to calm us down. After that they moved us to a car. We had seen cars outside our house, but didn't understand what it meant until that moment.

They put her into one of the cars, and a few minutes later they moved us into the other car. They always used two cars in a kidnapping. We just drove and drove. It was years later, when I came back to Guatemala, that I discovered the place that they took us to. In Guatemala City there are a lot of police stations, and we were taken to one downtown. I don't remember too much; you don't want to remember, so you block a lot of things out. But mostly I remember the sounds of people screaming. There were other people besides us being detained and tortured in this place. I remember darkness, and the walls were really dirty with blood, that smell of copper. We were there for a long time. They would put our heads inside buckets of cold water. You feel like you're drowning inside the bucket. They had a big box of cockroaches and they would put us in there and try to shut us inside, laugh about it, and take us out again. Those were the kinds of things that happened there.

My mother was present the whole time. She would just look at us and try to send us a lot of love in spite of what we were all experiencing. After that I don't remember. I remember going to sleep, shutting my eyes, and feeling really far away. All of a sudden someone would open my eyes with their fingers and shine a flashlight in my eyes and say to the other person, "No, she's okay." So I know there were doctors at these places, just to monitor how far the torture could go, to see if the person were able to be tortured more or if that's enough. The next memory I have is of being back at home. We were placed on the bed, and both of us woke up at the same time. It was morning again. My brother got up and looked around the house. Soon he came back and said, "There's no one here. We should go." I said, "Okay." We were dressed already, really dirty and stuff, but we didn't take anything—we just walked out. I said to him, "I forgot my sweater," thinking that my mom would be angry because we were always supposed to go out with our sweaters. He gave me a "Who cares about the sweater!" look. We just looked at each other.

We went outside the front door to let our neighbour know what was happening. She looked really scared and just said, "You have to run, you have to run!" We didn't understand; we didn't realize that everyone knew what was happening, because the police had raided the whole neighbourhood. They were up on the roofs of everyone's houses. We just looked at each other, held hands, and began to run. And the cars that had been there the day my mom was kidnapped began to follow us. We heard the wheels screech, but because we were used to playing hide-and-seek, we knew all the spaces between the houses where cars couldn't go, and this knowledge enabled us to get out of the neighbourhood. We ended up at our aunt's house with the idea of telling her what was happening. When we got there she said, "Oh, finally you're here, get in the car!" We drove out of the city and switched into another car, and we just drove to another province. We were there for two or three years until we were able to go up to Canada.

The day my mother was kidnapped, my father had stopped at the corner store to buy tortillas on his way home from work. The ladies working there told him, "Don't go to your house. The whole neighbourhood is raided and they're specifically in your home." He was very scared and didn't know what to do. He called a lot of people he knew—reporters, judges, doctors, other professionals—in the hope that he could get someone to accompany him to the house and take us out. Everyone he talked to said, "You know what? We'll give you money, help to get you out of the country—anything but that. We are not going in there." They told him, "Your wife is there, your children are there, and if your children live they are going to need one parent. If you go in there, they are going to be without either." So he had to make that decision. He had no other choice.

He ended up taking refuge in one of the embassies for a few days. They asked him where he wanted to go. He wanted to stay, but they told him he had to go or they would kill him, so they sent him to Canada. It took two or three years for immigration to accept his case and to get permission for my brother and me to come up and join him.

FIONA: How was life in Vancouver?

WENDY: In Vancouver everything was really hard, especially for my father. For us kids, learning the language and getting accustomed to the culture wasn't so difficult because we were a lot younger. We went to high school there, and later on I began to participate in the Vancouver Latino theatre group, and that is what changed my life. Theatre of the Oppressed taught me how to apply its techniques to my life. Years later I met another woman from Argentina who began to tell me about a group there called HIJOS, who were all sons or daughters of people who had disappeared during the dictatorship. They were doing a lot of great work around memory and justice.

I always wanted to go back to Guatemala. When my mom was kidnapped, I remember looking at the soldiers and trying to remember their faces. I would just stare at them and say to myself, "When I'm older I'm going to come back and I'm going to look for them." I would try to remember everything—their faces, gestures, heights. With my theatre work, I felt I could move back, and that is exactly what I did in 1999. I met my family again and I shared my ideas about doing popular theatre and human rights work with them. They said, "Yes, let's go to the university, where there are a lot of people who are very active."

Closing the Cycle of Death

WENDY: During the time we were preparing and organizing, the military diary was made public in Guatemala. It contained the names, photos, and descriptions of people kidnapped during the war. A soldier had stolen the diary from the military archives, gone to the US, and sold it to the National Security Archives. People came from El Salvador to see if their relatives' names were listed in the documents. The children and relatives of the disappeared were not allowed to go into the room where the archives were kept, and waiting outside gave us a chance to talk to other affected youth, to share stories, photos, and memories. A lot of our initial activities focused on sharing stories, memories of our parents, the songs they liked, the games they played, and so on. At one point we realized that we needed to be a public organization.

We decided that Military Day, celebrated annually on June 30, would be an appropriate day to make the existence of our group public. The decision to come out on Military Day started out as a joke when we said to one another, "Oh, wouldn't it be great if we disrupted Military Day to tell them that we are not going to let them forget?" And everyone laughed so much! And then we looked at each other and said, "That's the best idea we've had so far!" We made a banner and painted our faces, created some songs. And we came out. Now, some human rights organizations had already held protests near the parade. But we decided we had to get up really close, and in their faces. We needed them to see us. We wanted them to hear us. Because the military families also attend the parade, we decided that would be the safest place for us to be. During the parade, we began to inch up closer and closer, until all of us stood in the front line. Once President Álvaro Arzú began his speech, we launched into our songs and unrolled our banners. Nobody knew about HIJOS yet, and of course he was a little shocked and confused. Arzú had to improvise what he was saying, and I remember him referring to us, saying, "Oh, we've just begun peace in Guatemala. You can't enter into peace with confrontation." We yelled back at him that we couldn't walk into peace without justice.

We were really, really happy about this action, and ever since we have been working a lot around memory, justice, impunity, and silence in Guatemala. We began holding workshops at high schools and universities, and with different community groups on themes related to youth, loss, and the recuperation of historical memory. Most of us are popular educators and into popular theatre. We talk about what happened during the war, what the consequences were. What are the effects that we're still seeing now? We work a lot with art, especially participatory mural projects with communities. We think that culture and education are really the things that are going to push big social, political, and cultural changes in Guatemala now. We don't have money. We don't have the media. But we have our own tools: culture and education.

Every time we work with murals, people always say, "Oh, I just feel so good now." They say things like, "Last night after we did the mural I dreamt about my mom, but not what happened when they kidnapped her. I dreamt about the time when we were okay." We met with other communities and spoke with them—not just about what had happened during the war, but also about the present, and that led us to work on other pressing political issues. We talked a lot about the globalization of commerce and neoliberalism, and how this was going to affect the communities.

We soon started to connect with other youth organizations. Right now we are participating in a coalition of groups called Bloque Anti-Imperialista [the Anti-Imperialist Bloc]. We are one of the organizations that bring historical memory into political work, because we think it is a tool for resistance. Through this approach, we have been able to strengthen not just our organization, but other political groups, too, because we try to bring an analysis of where the problems come from and how we can begin to understand the larger structural roots of violence, trauma, loss, and fear, which are such big parts of life in post-war Guatemala. In 2004, for example, over several months we held a big celebration—in the form of a denunciation—of the fifty-year anniversary of the US invasion of Guatemala, an event that changed the country forever.

FIONA: Can you talk a little about the kinds of practices involved in recuperating historical memory?

WENDY: Ever since we came out, HIJOS has been working around the recuperation of historical memory in different ways. Sometimes people in the broader community ask us to organize a tribute to one of their family members who was killed, or to a village where a massacre was perpetrated during the war, and we help them organize those events. Treasured personal photographs of the victims are always good to work with. We often work with other personal items, too: a special scarf, a guitar, shoes, earrings, or a necklace associated with the person we are commemorating. We present the item in an exposition where people can talk about it. Sometimes people ask us to write poems or do theatre pieces for them. We also sometimes do work around the clandestine cemeteries. For example, if there is a family member or a neighbour who remembers the location of a mass grave, we begin a whole process of finding the cemetery, removing all the bones, and having a ceremony to bury the victims again. It then becomes a place for memory, a place where the victims' loved ones can take flowers, talk to them, or whatever. It is something that really helps us. They aren't our own family members, but to have someone else find theirs is a very healing process for all of us. It is a way of closing the cycle of death.

Women's Public Struggle against Fear

WENDY: In 2001, human rights activist Rigoberta Menchú presented a case to the Spanish court on the massacres carried out by the military during the war. Other communities soon joined her effort—organizations of the disappeared from the 1970s, the 1980s, and then us from the 1990s onwards. So we had three generations of activist groups working on behalf of the disappeared coming together to make our case on behalf of our loved ones. It is important for us to acknowledge the history of struggle that these generations of activist groups have given us. Most of the activists have been women, which is really important in Guatemala.

FIONA: Why is the role of women in the movement particularly important?

WENDY: Because the culture generally tends to exploit women, and because when their children or husbands disappeared, women changed totally. After that, their lives started taking place in the streets. They would chain themselves to the national palace, demanding the release of their children. Now many of these women activists say, "We were born from our children," not the other way around. Because now they are political, they are public and active in the streets, yelling, which is something that does not normally happen in Guatemala. Sometimes they did this without the support of the men of the community. People said it was dangerous, that it would come back to hurt the men. But the women said, "No, I have to do this. It's my child, my husband, my brother."

FIONA: Do you think the presence of women had an impact on how people saw that struggle?

WENDY: Yes, because people who work around human rights are seen as crazy in Guatemala. The media especially and the authorities treat them this way, and then the people in general will say, "Oh, they're crazy, maybe they're going through menopause," or "They have nothing to do." They say this even though their husbands have disappeared!

HIJOS is usually portrayed in the media that way: "Oh, those poor guys! They grew up with all these crazy women, their parents." And the military generals will say this too when they are brought to testify. They will say things like, "You know what? Stop fucking crying. Your mother or father is probably in Mexico, in Cancun taking a nice vacation, in Cuba on the beaches, so don't come to us because they don't love you." Forty-five thousand people were disappeared in Guatemala during the war.

The peace accords brought a little breathing space, but once the post–peace accord UN mission left Guatemala in 1999, things got difficult again, because the government really doesn't want to fulfill what the peace accords said. Over ten years have passed and they have done nothing. The situation is in many ways even worse now than during the war. There is a huge disparity between the poor and the rich. The justice system is in terrible shape; impunity is rampant. In the 1970s and 1980s there was still a process of justice in Guatemala. But in the last twenty years, the situation has deteriorated. People have to present their own cases. I've gone to present cases and officials of the court will say things like, "Do you really want to pursue this? Because nothing is going to happen here." They know, because they're the ones in power. That's the level of impunity. And that's why relatives and community members have to go to the international courts, like Rigoberta Menchú did in Spain.

The courts are just one space that we need to open up. HIJOS is also working on creating a video archive of children of the disappeared, so we'll have a video record of the people who survived in Guatemala. Up until now the government, and especially the military, have never accepted what they did. For them, genocide was never committed in Guatemala. There's a risk that because they won the war they will write its history, so we want to make sure that there are other sources of information that people will have access to, so that no one will ever say that genocide didn't take place in Guatemala.

Well after the signing of the peace accords, the practice of forced disappearance continued in Guatemala. Two special cases stand out. One is the disappearance of Hector Reyes, who was a labour organizer from a place outside Guatemala City called Nueva Linda. He was a *campesino* [rural or peasant] community leader struggling for better labour conditions and rights to land for his family and neighbours. The other is the case of Oscar Duarte, a community leader in one of the marginalized communities in Guatemala City. His group was doing community development, such as trying to rid the community of dirty water, fighting for better education, and so on. Because of the impact these two men were having on their communities, they were both kidnapped and disappeared. The way the perpetrators took them mirrored the style used by the army and the intelligence services during the 1970s and 1980s. These two cases are still open. No bodies have been found. But people witnessed the kidnapping. Witnesses reported that the police saw it happen and did nothing.

FIONA: Do you have a sense of who is carrying out such disappearances today? Is it still the military or the police?

WENDY: Well, for example, in the case of Hector Reyes, we gather that a plantation owner was responsible. In the case of Oscar Duarte, apparently it was the police, because he was doing a lot of work around adolescents and youth, trying to get them out of the gangs. The police always assume youths are part of gangs, and there is a lot of police violence in these communities. There has been a lot of what they call "social cleansing," which means that certain powerful actors think the best way to get rid of gang members is to kill them, and because the police consider virtually all youth to be gang members, they become targets for police on the street.

FIONA: Why is historical memory an important arena in which to intervene in Guatemala's public reckoning about the war and its legacy?

WENDY: For us, talking about historical memory around forced disappearances and violence more generally is really important because we work a lot with youth, and most of the questions they ask go something like, "Why are we living like this?" or they say, "When we were born Guatemala was already like this, so nothing is ever going to change." But when we speak about historical memory with younger people, they go through a process of rescuing their own history and are able to identify that the present situation of pervasive violence has not always been this way. They learn how to think about and identify historical causes. Once you are able to identify some of the roots of systemic violence and injustice, you can change that situation, now and in the future.

Uncovering Histories

FIONA: HIJOS has developed a set of creative political practices devoted to uncovering what you call historical memory. Can you talk about what this practice looks like and how it relates to the movement's organizing around social and political justice more broadly?

WENDY: People don't always have the strength to resist, to organize in different ways. Through historical memory, which also encompasses collective and individual memory, we are able to rescue the example of people— men, women, youth, even children—who in different times of our history have brought profound change in Guatemala. So when we talk about the war and the genocide, we don't only speak about the victims and how they were killed and with what levels of barbarity they were massacred, tortured, or whatever. Mainly we speak about who they were as people in the world, asking questions like, "What did they do? What were their names? Who were their parents? What did they enjoy?" We also rescue historical memory, for example, around the objects that people had, books they read. Or sometimes we re-enact an activity that was particular to a person's life and identity. A father, for example, used to go for a run at six in the morning before going to work. So we would re-enact his run, take the same route at the same time of day, see what he saw, see what the street looked like when he was running. By doing this, we try to rescue the dignity of the person who was obliterated in the most unspeakable way.

During the war it was important for groups to concentrate on denouncing human rights violations. There was a lot of pain and horror in telling stories. But now that some time has passed, we can affirm ourselves as victims, but also as survivors. Although we lived through terror, and it is important to name it, it is also important to say, "I am alive now. I have the strength to do something about it now, and not just cry about our history." Naming and talking about what happened is important in order to heal, but after the pain, there is something else. If we are always stuck in our pain, we are not going to be able to understand what other feelings come next. So this combination of acts and attitude is the basis of the idea of historical memory for us.

In Guatemala up until now, neither the government nor the military has accepted that the state forces committed the genocide. A lot of people linked to the repression have been trying to deny that there was any genocide. They have been publishing books, opinion pieces, and articles, and speaking out across radio and television. This is very dangerous. They are the ones who won the war, and they are the ones who are writing its history. There is a risk that in a few generations they are going to be able to say that genocide was never committed at all. Because the war lasted so long, there are a lot of people who lived through the war that have already passed away, and nobody ever heard their testimonies. Those stories are gone.

We are interested in recovering these histories, and so we are working on recording how elders see this history as they look back now that they are seventy, eighty, or ninety years old. For example, we have been recording the stories of a man who participated in the overthrow of the thirty-year dictatorship in 1954. He was twenty-six years old and already a member of Congress. He survived the 1954 invasion, lived through the war and the ten years of the peace accords, and just turned ninety this year. He is a person who continues with the spirit of struggle with so much excitement, and we want to be like that!

De-militarizing the Mind

FIONA: This makes me think about the anthropologist Michael Taussig's writing about how state and corporate terror operate by making the world very difficult to understand, by making it incomprehensible. Confusion seems to be central to any strategy of terror in that it is difficult to discern a pattern to the fear, and this exacerbates the experience of trauma. To me, it sounds like HIJOS is trying to clear away some of that confusion, to bring clarity and shed a very bright, if painful, light on not just the past but also the present. How does that work as a political project?

WENDY: Yes, exactly. It has to work because it is necessary. That way people can make decisions about what they want out of their lives and how they can be involved in social change. It is difficult, though. Just today I received a message about a pronouncement made by an association of Guatemalan military veterans, most of them generals who participated in the genocide, calling on the public to support them. This pronouncement came a couple of weeks after the movement won a halt to the annual military parade. Suddenly they were not permitted to go on the streets and celebrate the genocide they committed. We keep asking, "What does it take to get these people to change their hearts and minds?"

This is the most difficult part. It is not just a matter of de-militarizing the minds of people in general, because once people understand that there are other ways of relating to one another and that we don't have to be scared all the time, it is obvious that they will choose that, because life will be better. But how do you change the mind of a general who committed genocide? And it's not just about those who committed genocide in the past, because the generation of army officials graduating today is being taught the same doctrine. If they're learning the same techniques, or even more effective ones, history is going to happen all over again.

FIONA: It is difficult to imagine how it is possible, considering how asymmetrical the power of force is between groups like HIJOS and the trained and equipped Guatemalan military, but do you think that the military is actually scared of the movement? Does it see the impunity it has enjoyed for so long threatened?

WENDY: Definitely. I think what scares them the most is the fact that when they were carrying out the massacres and disappearing our families, we were present. One, two, three, four, five-year-olds, nine-year-olds, witnessing what was happening. I think it never crossed their minds that these children were going to grow up and become conscious of what was happening. They did not think anyone would be demanding justice, memory, and truth. So yes, I think they are scared. They planned every detail about how to hide the crimes, but now all that control appears to be slipping out of their hands. A lot of clandestine cemeteries have been found with, for example, three hundred people who have since been buried with the proper ceremonies. So the truth has this way of slowly coming out. I think that is what they are scared of. We are a new generation, and we are not afraid. We have a lot of strength, a lot of creativity. We have learned from the past, from our parents and how they organized in the universities, for example. But we also have new ways of organizing that are appropriate to our contemporary culture, our subculture. So I think they are scared of that.

Our Love Is Bigger Than Their Fear

FIONA: Do the consequences or possible outcomes of your dedicated, pacific agitation scare you, too?

WENDY: Yes. I think there is a fear among all of us, and in some ways I believe history is repeating itself with us personally, especially because now some of us have children. I think there is a natural fear of the thought that maybe it will happen all over again, especially because the perpetrators have not changed. Among our group, we have spoken extensively about this, and we believe that the love we have for our family members and for anyone who was a victim or survivor of the war, in Guatemala or other parts of the world, is so much bigger than any fear that they can throw at us. That love and respect that we have is way bigger than any fear they may inject into us. Sometimes we ask ourselves, "Would my mother go through the same struggle if I had been the one who disappeared?" And the answer is yes, without a doubt. So now we can ask, would the 250,000 people who were killed during the war do something about what was happening? Yes, definitely. If they had a second chance, they would be doing the same kind of work. So we also understand that it's not just for us, but also for other people.

Letting the Walls Speak

FIONA: Can you talk more about HIJOS's use of images, graphics, and art in general? Do you see the city as a kind of canvas for the restoration of historical memory? How does this infrastructure provide a space for interpreting the present through the eyes of history's survivors?

WENDY: Well, we love to do graffiti and paint murals on the street. It all began because in Guatemala there is so little information in the mainstream media about what is happening in the country, or internationally, for that matter. Exterior walls are like the newspapers of ordinary people.

We were not the first to use this communication tactic. Activists in the 1960s used charcoal to speak through the walls. People would take it from their kitchen and while out on protest marches or coming and going from work in the morning, they would write something on the wall, like "We are hungry, we need food. We want water. We want education." Later on, as people gained access to other materials, they would use thick paintbrushes and black paint. We use spray paint, stencils, paper, glue, and so on. Once we had become a lot better at communicating through walls, we started using stencils. People really appreciated it, because the pressures of day-to-day life are intense, especially if you're rushing to work, running for the bus, and so on, and all of a sudden you see a graffito that reflects the feelings that touch you daily, like "We should be getting paid more." Simple, just that.

Other symbols speak to more specific aspects of Guatemalan history. For example, one stencil we made was a silhouette of a police officer with a machine gun with the words, "I was trained in the School of the Americas to kill." A few days later the same stencils appeared on the walls with different text that another collective had added to it. And in another instance, on the same stencil, someone else added to the dialogue. They applied red spray paint to the tip of the police's gun and let it drip. Last year we were celebrating the birthday of Che Guevara and we made stencils with the traditional photo of him wearing the hat emblazoned with a star. About a week later someone else made the same stencil, but with different haircuts. In one he looked like Jesus Christ. In another he had a mohawk, and in another he had a red nose like a clown. It was great! Really wonderful. Sometimes the government, especially the mayor of Guatemala City, will try to clean up all the graffiti, especially if it is political. They hire people to paint over it at night. One guy who had been hired to paint over our graffiti subverted the censorship by tracing his brush exactly over what we had written. So, for example, we had painted "JUSTICE" on a wall and he used the same colour paint, but different by just a tone or two, and traced right over the words. When the employer admonished him, he just said, "I painted over it!"

FIONA: It is so interesting how many layers of non-coordinated collaboration take place in a single act of political art! It sounds like your use of graffiti is a way to comment on ongoing political and social events and debates, while also providing an interesting commentary on the impenetrability of the commercial media. You have to use the walls because this is the only media infrastructure that is available. Can you tell me about the more deliberate and long-term mural projects that HIJOS undertakes with small, rural villages and peripheral urban communities?

WENDY: This is an important part of our work. We make murals in communities, and through this we engage in a process of dialogue about collective memory. It starts with communities in both rural and urban areas telling us what type of mural they want on their walls. We visit the community and start by asking, "What do you guys remember about the war?" From there, a community discussion begins. People have different memories and feelings about the war and want different aspects of their experience represented in the murals. People begin to put images, photographs, feelings, or stories into different images, whether it be a flower, a colour, or something like that. For example, people will say things like, "Let's have blue, because the skies are clear and we want to clear our minds, because they are always blue." The murals will usually be placed in either a home or an abandoned house. Because people have participated in creating them, they take care of the murals. Sometimes you see a neighbour with a machete cleaning up the weeds growing around it.

We also do murals of our own when we see a really nice wall. There are a number of walls that you pass when entering downtown Guatemala City that are in dispute. Ever since HIJOS was born, we've done murals on one of those walls—a huge, beautiful wall. Across the street is a shantytown, a community of people living in cardboard and nylon houses. Whenever the residents of this community see us out there painting, they always come and help us out, asking if we need water, suggesting techniques for painting, asking if they can paint something. They call us sometimes to tell us, "You guys have to get down here. They are painting over your mural!" Then we go there to see who is responsible for covering it up. At first we thought it was the military, but then we discovered it was the mayor's office. There could be a mural from one of the gangs—like MS or the Eighteenth Street—and they would not cover it up. But it is clear that because our graffiti makes claims like "justice for genocide," they want it gone. There is one wall we have painted about ten murals on, and the city always paints over them. We go back when we have enough money, or when someone gives us paint, and make a new one. There are different walls throughout the city and in parts of the countryside that are in dispute.

Fearless Speech

FIONA: It sounds like you have to work fast and be ready to see all your work vanish overnight. How long do you take to make a mural? What kinds of themes do you usually take up in your graffiti and murals?

WENDY: We take about four days to paint a mural if we are putting it someplace, like a school, where we know they won't paint over it. If we know there is a risk of the mayor painting over it, then we will work on a mural for about four to six hours.

Often the graffiti will say things like "Justice for genocide—we all know who killed everyone in Guatemala." A few blocks later, we will have another instalment with the answer: "The Guatemalan army." Downtown there are many streets that are only one way, which is useful for this technique. Some graffiti will start with something alarming, like, "We have to re-arm ourselves," and two blocks later will appear, ". . . with hope, with dignity." These are meant to get you thinking. We may share different critiques about free trade agreements. Or in the shantytowns closer to downtown, we may put something like, "Welcome middle class, you're all welcome here." Others ask questions to the public, to urge them to think about how much the political class earns and how little the rest of us are paid.

Sometimes we refer to the legacy of the war: "The forced disappearances in Guatemala have not disappeared; impunity perpetuates them." And we try to point out the ongoing impunity enjoyed by specific criminals in the military, such as [ex–military dictator] General Ríos Montt. One of our stencils featured an enormous image of Montt's face, which we coupled with a line from a poem by Pablo Neruda: "For the one that gave the order of torture, I ask for a sentence." Sometimes we will use a quote from Otto René Castillo, a Guatemalan writer who was disappeared in the 1960s, or other figures that symbolize the strength to struggle for change. Sometimes we write things as though these writers composed them.

It may sound like a small thing, but since the start, we have always signed our graffiti. This is more common now, but it was never done before. People thought that you shouldn't identify yourself when you speak so openly and in opposition to the government. But that doesn't help! We are not a clandestine organization; we are a public organization, so it is important for us to identify ourselves. During the war, people had so much fear of identifying themselves as oppositional or leftist thinkers that now people, especially the older generations, continue with that idea. They say, "You have to be careful, we have to be more quiet." And we say, "No; silence has been living in Guatemala for too long. And we don't want to be part of that. That's how you guys did it and it worked for you. But today, this is how the new generations are doing it." We want to be open.

FIONA: It is another way of saying, "We are still here!" Such a position strikes at the heart of HIJOS's political intervention. The members of HIJOS, after all, quite literally embody a history of struggle and resistance, and in that sense your very beings, your presence in public space, evoke collective memory. But it is still very dangerous, as the threats against your group and others involved in agitating for a different kind of society attest to. Does it make you feel more protected or somewhat safer to convey your public presence?

WENDY: I don't think it has anything to do with safety. It is more to do with our efforts to teach the older generations that we have to identify ourselves and not be afraid to say, "I think like a leftist and I want to act according to those principles for the rest of my life." Being public in this way says we won't separate ourselves from what we write, and by doing this we refuse to fall into the game of saying what we think only when it is convenient and of speaking up only if we know we won't get in trouble for it. You have to be open and frank with people. You have to let people know where you stand, and if you disagree, it's okay. You can sometimes see disagreements and conflicts among organizations in the graffiti.

FIONA: So political debates are playing out on public walls?

WENDY: Yes, and for HIJOS, when we sign our graffiti it also lets people know that we can disagree on some things and agree on a lot of things, too. I think the older generation doesn't really know how to deal with that, because they had to be so careful. Newer generations are more willing to debate, and we're therefore more open to thinking about conflict as a tool. If nothing else, it allows you to know a person better, and we have gotten to know ourselves better. Some people say we're way too direct, and we've been asked not to do graffiti or other kinds of actions. But conflict is healthy. It is useful for understanding where we want to go politically, socially, and so on. That we are asked not to is really scary.

FIONA: Do you see your wall art playing a role in reclaiming the city, in opening spaces for dialogue?

WENDY: Our graffiti work relates directly to our work in reclaiming the memory of the disappeared, as well as the city itself. This is why we plant our graffiti in symbolically significant places. For example, sometimes we make mosaics of people and glue a kind of plaque on the wall where they were disappeared. The mosaic provides an explanation of what happened. People react well to this. Parents picking their kids up from school will see one at a bus stop and the kids will always ask, "Who is that?" and the parents will explain that there was a war. Just to have that little space is an opening. Sometimes people will say they knew the person portrayed on the mosaic. Or if the person was a poet or a musician, that they knew them in a different way. The artwork brings out memories. Upon encountering it, people begin to talk, connecting the person on the mosaic with their own lives and memories.

INDEX

abolition of the death penalty, 14, 29–32
Abu-Jamal, Mumia, 29, 30, 31; *Live from Death Row*, 30
activism, and unity, 26–27, 144. *See also* social movements; youth activism
Africa, 41–43, 45, 47, 77, 96. *See also* specific countries
aggression, male, 113, 122
Albion's Fatal Tree (Hay, Linebaugh, Rule, Thompson, and Winslow), 16
Alianza Politica Sector de Mujeres (Political Alliance of the Women's Sector), 112, 134, 135–36, 137, 139, 141, 143
alter-globalization movement, 21, 33, 38, 112–13, 137, 143–4
alternative media, 2, 98, 155
alternative social relations, 13, 17, 19, 160–61. *See also* alternatives to the state; capitalism: alternatives to; Zapatistas
alternatives to capitalism. *See under* capitalism
alternatives to the state, 153–54
American Revolution, 15
Amnesty International, 142
anger, 45, 128, 131–32, 139, 166. *See also* rage
animals and humans, 48–49, 51–52
anti-capitalism, 86, 94, 95–98, 100, 105–6, 109–14, 116, 151, 157–58, 160–61; struggles against and beyond capitalism, 98–99, 110–11, 113, 114
anti-colonial movement, 40, 54, 76, 77–78

anti-corporate legislation, 69
anti-fascist movement. *See* World War II resistance movements
anti-fear. *See under* fear
anti-imperialism, 171. *See also* anti-colonial movement
anti-migration. *See under* migration
anti-trafficking. *See* human trafficking
anti-war movement, 62–63, 90
anti–white slave movement, 86
apartheid, 77, 92, 93, 94
APPO (Popular Assembly of the Peoples of Oaxaca), 154–55
Arbenz Guzmán, Jacobo, 140, 165
Arendt, Hannah, 2
Argentina, 96, 98, 99, 111, 125, 137, 169
Ariès, Philippe, 52
art and activism, 2, 7, 9, 139, 163, 164, 169–71, 179–80, 183. *See also* graffiti and murals; theatre
Arzú, Álvaro, 170
assassination, 61, 140, 148
Atlantic history, 9, 14, 16, 20, 21, 54–55
austerity, 1, 6, 70, 75, 96; imposed by World Bank and IMF, 34, 41. *See also* structural adjustment: imposed by governments
automobile industry, 67, 68
Autonomist Marxism, 33, 95
Autonomous University of Puebla, 95
asymmetrical power, 66, 112–13, 177